Sacred Moments
A Pause with God

The Reverend Doctor Deborah Kaiser-Cross

Photography by David Middleton

Creative Director   Laurie Bohlke

Editors   Lynn Hughes and Sally Watkins

Scripture quotations marked (ESV) are from the ESV® Bible (The Holy Bible, English Standard Version®), copyright © 2001 by Crossway, a publishing ministry of Good News Publishers. Used by permission. All rights reserved.

Scripture quotations marked (NIV) are taken from the Holy Bible, New International Version®, NIV®. Copyright © 1973, 1978, 1984, 2011 by Biblica, Inc.™ Used by permission of Zondervan. All rights reserved worldwide. www.zondervan.com The "NIV" and "New International Version" are trademarks registered in the United States Patent and Trademark Office by Biblica, Inc.™

Scripture marked (NKJV) are taken from the New King James Version®. Copyright © 1982 by Thomas Nelson. Used by permission. All rights reserved.

Scripture quotations marked (NLT) are taken from the Holy Bible, New Living Translation, copyright ©1996, 2004, 2007, 2013 by Tyndale House Foundation. Used by permission of Tyndale House Publishers, Inc., Carol Stream, Illinois 60188. All rights reserved.

Scripture quotations marked (NRSV) are taken from the New Revised Standard Version Bible, copyright 1989, Division of Christian Education of the National Council of the Churches of Christ in the United States of America. Used by permission. All rights reserved.

Scripture quotations marked (The Message) are taken from THE MESSAGE. Copyright © by Eugene H. Peterson 1993, 1994, 1995, 1996, 2000, 2001, 2002. Used by permission of Tyndale House Publishers, Inc.

Scripture quotations marked (The Voice) taken from The Voice™. Copyright © 2008 by Ecclesia Bible Society. Used by permission. All rights reserved.

ISBN 978-1-889937-19-9
Published by Crescent Hill Books, Louisville, Kentucky
Book design: Hill Harcourt, Ashton Advertising, Louisville, Kentucky
Printed in China by Everbest through Four Colour Print Group, Louisville, Kentucky

Cover image: Grand Tetons, Wyoming
For more information on David Middleton's photography, visit his website: davidmiddletonphoto.com.

Dedication

To my fellow pilgrims at Jupiter First Church who make ministry such a joy and a delight

To my dear friend, Laurie Bohlke, whose passionate commitment and loving encouragement nudged this project to completion

To my husband, David, and to our children, who claim such a huge piece of my heart—Anne, Chad, Sarah and Michael—my life is full because of your love.

The language in this book of prayers is intended to reflect the many facets of God's deeply personal nature, revealed in images that are both masculine and feminine. Each one of us has particular favorite ways of addressing God. As you read each of these prayers, please use any salutation that brings you closer to God.

Acknowledgments

Recognizing that every creative project has been crafted by many unseen hands, I want to celebrate the gifts of some special people.

Pausing in gratitude to the following:

My mother whose constant affirmation helped me to trust that I could do all things in Christ

Lynn Hughes and Sally Watkins who took my words and enhanced them with their careful editing

David Middleton, Claire Beck, Brenda Berry, Bill Bohlke, Laurie Bohlke, Tisa Queen-Oldham, and Jeff Wendorff whose abilities to capture nature's miracles through the lens of a camera brought the words to life

Barbara Johnson and Lynn Hughes whose sensitivity to the choice of a perfect Scriptural verse to complement the prayers enhanced the whole project

Jennifer Bird, Barbara Johnson, Amy Jurskis, Reverend Jim Poppell, and Bill and JoAnn Potter who carefully reviewed the manuscript and added their wise reflections

Claire Beck, Michael Middleton, and Kristen Natelson who reviewed early versions of the manuscript and images

Bill Bohlke, our hidden hero, who contributed his editing wisdom from the beginning to the end of the project

Nancy Heinonen of Four Colour Print Group who facilitated the entire publishing and printing process

Hill Harcourt of Ashton Advertising whose attention to the graphic design and layout, to both beauty and detail, brought this book to life.

In the busyness of life, it may seem like a waste of time to slow down, to stop what I'm doing and spend time with God. I am learning that it is no more a waste of time than stopping to put gas in my car when it's almost empty. It is necessary. Pausing for a sacred moment with God creates more time, more joy, and more energy in my life.

O Lord, in my daily routines, when I pause and seek You, again and again You come to me in a sacred moment:

a chance word,

a casual conversation,

an image from the past,

the refrain of a praise song,

a stirring of prayer in the heart.

In that moment, Lord, You grant the miracle of peace, and I feel renewed. O Prince of Peace, let serenity dwell in the deepest parts of my soul. May your peace that passes all understanding take root and grow in the most unsettled spots of my world that I might see glimpses of your Kingdom here on earth.

JANUARY 1

O Lord of all, I celebrate the fresh mercies of this dawn—the sunbursts of morning light washing over the horizon, mingling with the symphony of nature to greet a brand new year. I come into your presence, Lord, with gratitude for all that You have done in my life in this past year. I am aware of the possibility of a fresh beginning in my spiritual life. Lead me in ways that might draw me closer to You, in ways that open me up more freely to your redeeming love. Let this be the year when I dare to invite You to sweep through my soul, revealing the best of who I am, while gently blowing the chaff away.

And I will give you a new heart, and I will put a new spirit in you. I will take out your stony, stubborn heart and give you a tender, responsive heart. Ezekiel 36:26 New Living Translation (NLT)

Maine coast

JANUARY 2

Gracious God, I come into your presence with gratitude for all that You have done in my life in this past year. During this week that bridges the old and the new, I remember especially the people who have filled my life with a rich legacy of faith and joy, and I celebrate the events of this past year that have helped me change and grow. As I enter a year full of unknowns, I turn to You in trust, believing it will be filled with possibility and hope—because You are the Lord of my life.

May the God of hope fill you with all joy and peace as you trust in him, so that you may overflow with hope by the power of the Holy Spirit.
Romans 15:13 New International Version (NIV)

How do I want to become closer to God this year?

JANUARY 3

O God of the morning star and sun showers, thank you yet again for the wonders of creation—a universe of amazing complexity, a planet created to support many lives—an artist's masterpiece that inspires me to praise You, the Creator of it all. On this Sabbath morning, I take the time to offer gratitude to You for the incredible blessings of life. As I create my own gratitude list, help me to remember that my blessings reach much deeper than mere possessions. Help me to abide in You so that my whole life is lived in thanksgiving. Whether I am in the midst of difficulties or in the sweetness of celebration, I will remain one of your grateful people.

The Lord is good to everyone.
He showers compassion on all his creation.
All of your works will thank you, Lord,
and your faithful followers will praise you.
Psalm 145:9-10 (NLT)

My blessings include . . .

JANUARY 4

O Lord of great compassion, as I open the pages of this new year, I find myself trembling at the unknown. I carry too many fears that never come to pass, and I find myself wasting my life away in worry. Gracious God, I pray that your comfort might so deeply abide within me that any lingering fears might be blown away with the whisper of the wind of your Holy Spirit, and I would know the peace that comes from trusting You moment by moment.

But I'll take the hand of those who don't know the way,
 who can't see where they're going.
I'll be a personal guide to them,
 directing them through unknown country.
I'll be right there to show them what roads to take,
 make sure they don't fall into the ditch.
These are the things I'll be doing for them —
 sticking with them, not leaving them for a minute.
Isaiah 42:16 (The Message)

Pine marten, Vermont

JANUARY 5

One of the treasures of my Trinitarian faith is this: I believe that God is with me—not just as a Father in heaven who loves me; and not simply as Jesus the Christ who came to show me the way to the Father's heart; but also as the Holy Spirit with me today as close as my breath. In the Bible, the word for the Holy Spirit in both Hebrew and Greek is *breath*. As I take each breath, inhaling and exhaling, I am celebrating God with me in this very moment.

Dear Lord, I sense the unmistakable touch of your Spirit right now. In this moment I offer You the thoughts that sometimes overwhelm me. Grant me eyes with the vision to see beyond any present situation so that I can see your will unfold all around me.

One day when the crowds were being baptized, Jesus himself was baptized. As he was praying, the heavens opened, and the Holy Spirit, in bodily form, descended on him like a dove. And a voice from heaven said, "You are my dearly loved Son, and you bring me great joy." Luke 3:21-22 (NLT)

I breathe in and celebrate . . .

JANUARY 6

O Lord of all creation, who has fashioned every living thing with exquisite care, thank you that You chose to make me in your own image—for giving me the remarkable capacity to love with abandon, to forgive with freedom, to live with gusto, and to laugh with unrestrained joy. Yet so often, I neglect those very opportunities to abide in the fullness of life that You offer to me in Jesus. Re-orient my purpose and my priorities this morning to reflect yours.

But let all who take refuge in you be glad;
*   let them ever sing for joy.*
Spread your protection over them,
*   that those who love your name may rejoice in you.*
Psalm 5:11 (NIV)

I love to laugh when . . ..

JANUARY 7

O God of understanding, I bring to You the inner conflicts of my heart—my anxieties, my painful memories, my ruptured relationships, my unrealized dreams. During my most difficult times, when my carefully ordered world seems to fall apart, it is You who ignites my hope, one flame at a time, bringing peace to the injured places in my soul. Your gift of hope is the anchor strong enough to hold my life together. With it, O Lord, my dreams never have to perish.

We can rejoice, too, when we run into problems and trials, for we know that they help us develop endurance. And endurance develops strength of character, and character strengthens our confident hope of salvation. And this hope will not lead to disappointment. For we know how dearly God loves us, because he has given us the Holy Spirit to fill our hearts with his love.
Romans 5:3-5 (NLT)

Minturn, Colorado

JANUARY 8

Lord of the dreamer, I celebrate the visions that You have planted deep within me, and I rejoice that You do exceedingly more than I could ever ask or imagine. In this time of prayer, I quiet myself long enough to remember that You alone are the God of miracle and majesty. Empower me and launch me into service. Help me to embrace the excitement of risk-taking, the exhilaration of the unknown, and the sheer joy of an adventure with You.

Now to him who by the power at work within us is able to accomplish abundantly far more than all we can ask or imagine, to him be glory in the church and in Christ Jesus to all generations, forever and ever. Amen.
Ephesians 3:20-21 New Revised Standard Version (NRSV)

Where is God calling me to take a risk?

JANUARY 9

As I turn to You, Lord, I ask that You would calm the clattering of my mind so that I can be still and simply know that You are God, and I am not. Whatever I carry deep within me that needs your restoration, I trust in your promise that You will forgive me and help me to accept the freedom to move on, with yesterdays behind me and your hope before me. Set me on a path that honors You.

Trust in the LORD with all your heart;
  do not depend on your own understanding.
Seek his will in all you do,
  and he will show you which path to take.
Proverbs 3:5-6 (NLT)

I want to move on from . . .

JANUARY 10

God of the heavens, You graciously stand at the door of my heart, waiting for me to invite You in. Even when I am too busy to listen, You are always there, with open arms, ready to receive me with your unconditional acceptance and love. I bow my head in reverence and intentionally open my heart and mind to You, in awe of your great faithfulness, as You continually pour out your Spirit of goodness and grace. In response to your invitation, I joyfully welcome You who knows every thought, every want, every weakness—every aspect of my being—and yet so graciously loves me anyway.

Look! I stand at the door and knock. If you hear my voice and open the door, I will come in, and we will share a meal together as friends.
Revelation 3:20 (NLT)

Anguilla

JANUARY 11

Loving God, I am grateful for the countless ways You nudge me—sometimes gently and sometimes firmly—into opportunities for growth. You encourage me through situations that invite me to dare something new as I step out in faith. At other times, You seem to be at work in the midst of my toughest challenges. Your grace enfolds me as I am but also encourages me to become the person You have always envisioned me to be.

As I begin to embrace new attitudes and behaviors, O Lord, You have a way of taking me out of my comfort zone and leading me into wide-open spaces that sometimes feel scary and overwhelming. Yet, You are still the Lord of the journey, who has promised to lead me into broad expanses of living. As this new year unfolds, help me to be brave enough to try "different."

The disciples came up and asked, "Why do you tell stories?"
He replied, "You've been given insight into God's kingdom. You know how it works. Not everybody has this gift, this insight; it hasn't been given to them. Whenever someone has a ready heart for this, the insights and understandings flow freely. But if there is no readiness, any trace of receptivity soon disappears. That's why I tell stories: to create readiness, to nudge the people toward receptive insight. Matthew 13:10-13 (The Message)

I am called to . . .

JANUARY 12

A very wise woman, Corrie ten Boom, said, "Worry doesn't empty tomorrow of its troubles. It empties today of its strengths. Never be afraid to trust an unknown future to a known God."

All-merciful God, many times I carry concerns that need to be yielded to You and left in your hands, yet sometimes I feel as if You need to pry them from my clenched fists. Help me to release my concerns to You, trusting You with new steps in faith. As I envision the week ahead, I know I need your wisdom and presence. Let this be my prayer, Lord: lead me to be completely open to your will and your ways.

And we know that in all things God works for the good of those who love him, who have been called according to his purpose. Romans 8:28 (NIV)

What do I need to release?

JANUARY 13

O God of all glory, the gifts of creation encircle my senses. In these contemplative moments, memories surface reminding me of those carefree hours strolling along the beach, or drinking in the beauty of wide expanses of green, or daydreaming at noon as the light glows golden around me. It is in those attentive silences that your Holy Spirit speaks to me in so many ways beyond words, if I can listen with my heart. Help me to live in the silent spaces so that I might sense your word to me this day.

Listen, O heavens, and I will speak!
  Hear, O earth, the words that I say!
Let my teaching fall on you like rain;
  let my speech settle like dew.
Let my words fall like rain on tender grass,
  like gentle showers on young plants.
I will proclaim the name of the LORD;
  how glorious is our God!
Deuteronomy 32:1-3 (NLT)

Vancouver Island, Canada

JANUARY 14

Gracious God, when I consider your amazing mercy and grace, You give me the courage to face myself and know that my life has not always reflected your presence. I have disappointed You and those I love and have even rationalized my behavior, trying to convince myself that I had good reason for resisting your ways. I remember my impatience, my harsh words, my short temper, my cutting corners of integrity. And so I turn to You, trusting in your promise of forgiveness, knowing that it is your acceptance that frees me to begin all over again. Your Spirit hovers over my heart, releasing me from the prisons of my own making and granting me your peace.

Make a clean break with all cutting, backbiting, profane talk. Be gentle with one another, sensitive. Forgive one another as quickly and thoroughly as God in Christ forgave you. Ephesians 4:31-32 (The Message)

I ask for forgiveness for . . .

JANUARY 15

Most Holy God, I ask that You would give me the courage I need in the tempests of my life. I pray for friends who know

the regrets over tasks done or left undone,

the pain of words spoken without careful thought.

the worry of dealing with addictions in a myriad of forms,

and the uncertainty of unrevealed futures.

I release these burdens to You, trusting that You know exactly what each of your children needs in this moment in time. It is my deepest desire to be able to trust You with abandon, releasing each worry and every challenge to You, relying on your strength to see me through.

"I am the Lord, *the God of all the peoples of the world. Is anything too hard for me?* Jeremiah 32:27 (NLT)

I lift up these special concerns today . . .

JANUARY 16

Lord of the journey, help me to change this sometimes cold world around me with the warmth of your compassion. Instead of murmured complaints, grant me a vision of what could be different. Nourish within me a desire to build up rather than tear down and to risk rather than cling to security. Help me to walk on with the confidence that You are always with me.

This same Good News that came to you is going out all over the world. It is bearing fruit everywhere by changing lives, just as it changed your lives from the day you first heard and understood the truth about God's wonderful grace.
Colossians 1:6 (NLT)

Vermont

JANUARY 17

When I read the gospels, it's obvious that Jesus was always busy but never in a hurry. He never lacked things to do, but he didn't hurry through them. He was always present with people, body and soul.

O Lord, I seem to spend so much time focusing on distractions rather than on You. My thoughts are always on what I need to do and on situations that need attention. I am so seldom with You, in the moment, open to your presence. My mind flits elsewhere, and then I miss real life by not living in the moments You give me. I miss so much that I do not see, so many people I never touch, so many opportunities to offer grace. Remind me that tomorrow will take care of itself and that the abundant life You offer begins with You now in every moment of today.

So do not worry about tomorrow. Let tomorrow worry about itself. Living faithfully is a large enough task for today. Matthew 6:34 (The Voice)

Today I will try to live in the moment by . . .

JANUARY 18

Glorious God, as You send me forth into my ordinary life today, help me to be open to your promptings and to intentionally seek opportunities where I can serve You. Fill me so that I might give out of the overflow, and guide me so that I might venture with courage for the journey. I pray that I can become your love in action. May those gifts that are uniquely mine be used wisely and to your glory.

Now that I, your LORD and Teacher, have washed your feet, you also should wash one another's feet. I have set you an example that you should do as I have done for you. Very truly I tell you, no servant is greater than his master, nor is a messenger greater than the one who sent him. Now that you know these things, you will be blessed if you do them. John 13:14-17 (NIV)

How could I use my gifts today?

JANUARY 19

O Gentle Shepherd, I come seeking You in this sacred time of prayer yet find myself being found by You. How wonderfully rich my life is with You. Thank you for the countless ways You touch me, in the shimmering silver morning light across a pond, in a squirrel's playful circling of the trees, in the warm, knowing smile of a friend's welcome. Most of all, thank you for always being present when I open my heart to You in the silence of prayer.

Steep your life in God-reality, God-initiative, God-provisions. Don't worry about missing out. You'll find all your everyday human concerns will be met.
Matthew 6:33 (The Message)

Glacier National Park, Montana

JANUARY 20

Blessed Savior, help me to remember what is most important in life. And then help me to surrender my life more fully to your power as I
>   walk more slowly,
>>   live more simply,
>>>   and love more boldly.

Then I pray that You would enable me to be a blessing to those who cross my path, trusting Jesus to lead the way.

You will keep in perfect peace
  those whose minds are steadfast,
  because they trust in you.
Isaiah 26:3 (NIV)

With God's help I can . . .

JANUARY 21

Precious Lord, I yearn to grasp deeper truths that come only as I ponder life quietly and thoughtfully and seek your wisdom. Help me to draw closer to You. Breathe new hope and empower fresh life into my soul. Encourage me to live the sentiments of St. Francis—to preach the gospel of Jesus at all times, and if necessary, to use words. It is in and through Him that I live and pray.

My mouth will speak words of wisdom;
  the meditation of my heart will give you understanding.
Psalm 49:3 (NIV)

In what situations do I need God's wisdom?

JANUARY 22

Loving Lord, teach me to wait patiently with You day by day as I invite the power of your Spirit to refashion my life into an instrument of your grace. Teach me to see with new eyes the world You have created for me to enjoy. Lift the heavy weariness from my spirit and replace it with your abiding joy. Teach me to be fully present in each moment of my day. Increase my sensitivity to the people around me so that You might use my gifts to be a blessing to them in the name of Jesus.

Are you tired? Worn out? Burned out on religion? Come to me. Get away with me and you'll recover your life. I'll show you how to take a real rest. Walk with me and work with me—watch how I do it. Learn the unforced rhythms of grace. I won't lay anything heavy or ill-fitting on you. Keep company with me and you'll learn to live freely and lightly. Matthew 11:28-30 (The Message)

Land iguana, Galapagos

JANUARY 23

Compassionate God, I know that a life of faith doesn't save me from the hardships that are a part of being alive. But I also know that my faith grants me the opportunity to share my struggles with You, certain that You will hold both me and those that I care deeply about in your holy embrace. O Lord, help me to see You waiting for me in the darker valleys of life:

in a waiting room where words of anxiety are whispered in prayer,

in parts of this world where poverty and violence are part of daily life,

in hearts that are trying to cope with loss and addiction and hopelessness.

Help me to see your hand in all of life—so that I might experience the hope You offer to each person who reaches out to You this day in Jesus Christ.

You are my refuge and my shield;
I have put my hope in your word.
Psalm 119:114 (NIV)

I am hoping for . . .

JANUARY 24

Many years ago when our children were small, I was running around trying to do too much. One of our daughters caught my attention, took my face in her little hands, and said, "Listen to me with your eyes, Mama." I wonder how often God would like us to stop and pay attention, too.

O Lord of both the infinite and the infinitesimal, thank you for the blessings around me that are obvious—the moments when I notice the droplets dancing on rain puddles or crisp mornings that invigorate my spirit. I also thank you for blessings that might go unnoticed—the moment of awareness when your love is expressed through another person or a growing maturity in grace that is brand new for me. Thank you for blessings that might at first glance be hidden—those challenges that You have allowed to touch me which, at first, might appear as difficulties but ultimately are building my character.

I said, "Let days speak,
  and many years teach wisdom."
But truly it is the spirit in a mortal,
  the breath of the Almighty, that makes for understanding.
Job 32:7-8 (NRSV)

I want to be more aware of . . .

JANUARY 25

Slow my stride, O God, so that I might respond to your encouragement to rest awhile by your well and be filled with your living water. Give rest to my racing heart and bring calm to my harried feelings. Still my mind enough to savor the soothing sound of the surf or the morning sun reflecting on one dew-drenched leaf. Lead me from the rushing of my days of constant doing to the sitting here, experiencing the reward of simply being in your presence in this sacred moment.

The LORD will fight for you; you need only to be still. Exodus 14:14 (NIV)

Bill Bohlke

JANUARY 26

Wonderful, amazing God, You bless me with the beauty of my five senses, and today I celebrate the gift of touch. Thank you for the hands that have blessed me with a touch of understanding this week—a hug from an old friend, or the light reassurance of a hand on my shoulder when I needed it, or a stranger reaching out in welcome. Remind me that You often surprise me with your presence in the most unexpected places. So help me to notice, and then thank You for each hand that offers me the touch of Christ in my world this week.

When the people recognized Jesus, the news of his arrival spread quickly throughout the whole area, and soon people were bringing all their sick to be healed. They begged him to let the sick touch at least the fringe of his robe, and all who touched him were healed. Matthew 14:35-36 (NLT)

I could use the touch of Christ to . . .

Great God of wonders, You are the creative artist who has designed all that lies before me, both the inconceivable vastness of the galaxies of space and the tiny fingerprint of a newborn baby. I come to You with both honesty and my vulnerability. O God, I bring to You my many feelings because they are a real part of who I am—my burdens of anxiety, my painful memories, my simmering anger, and my unfinished dreams. I pray that You will comfort me as I share the truth of what I am experiencing in this moment.

Our actions will show that we belong to the truth, so we will be confident when we stand before God. Even if we feel guilty, God is greater than our feelings, and he knows everything. 1 John 3:19-20 (NLT)

What are some of God's unfinished dreams for me?

JANUARY 28

O Lord of this magnificent morning, I approach this day with gratitude for both the spectacular and the simple gifts around me—for crisp, clear mornings when sparkling new snow softly blankets my world, for storm-gathered clouds whipped by winds, and for that first glimpse of starlight in the evening sky. The stillness beckons me to delight in the silence in which You dwell. I lift your name on high and praise You for the song in my soul, the lift in my step, and the joy in my faith.

We were filled with laughter,
  and we sang for joy.
And the other nations said,
  "What amazing things the LORD has done for them."
Yes, the LORD has done amazing things for us!
  What joy!
Psalm 126:2-3 (NLT)

Vermont

JANUARY 29

O Lord of all, my unlimited source of sustenance, You provide rest, comfort, and refreshment when I call on your name. But I confess that I often go about my merry way with little thought of You and even neglect to acknowledge You. Yet I know that You are always by my side. Help me to hold fast to You in every hour and experience the joy of life lived with You.

As the Father has loved me, so have I loved you. Now remain in my love. If you keep my commands, you will remain in my love, just as I have kept my Father's commands and remain in his love. I have told you this so that my joy may be in you and that your joy may be complete. John 15:9-11 (NIV)

Today I can rest in God by . . .

JANUARY 30

Ever-present Lord, after these demanding few days, I pause to reflect with You. There were joys and achievements, but there were also frustrations and failures. As I reflect on my personal challenges, I pray that You would release me when I linger too long on what I cannot change, but allow me to imagine what I can yet be by trusting in your renewing love.

Praise the LORD,
  for he has heard my cry for mercy.
The LORD is my strength and my shield;
  my heart trusts in him, and he helps me.
My heart leaps for joy,
  and with my song I praise him.
Psalm 28:6-7 (NIV)

My personal challenge is . . .

Jupiter, Florida   Laurie Bohlke

Sometimes it's hard for me to make the transition from getting to worship to being in worship. I think about all I left behind and find it difficult to fully settle into being here in this place. A few thousand years ago, the Psalmist knew this and penned these words:

Enter his gates with thanksgiving
   and his courts with praise;
   give thanks to him and praise his name.

Psalm 100:4 (NIV)

The best way to make that transition to truly being here is through thanksgiving and worship.

Eternal God, thank you for all the ways I experience your infinite love through my family of faith. In worship, I see You in the warm smiles of those around me; I hear You in the music that fills my spirit; I am acutely aware of your presence as I explore the Word. I am grateful for the way I experience your love through the countless people who give selflessly to touch the lives of others in your name. Most of all, I am grateful for the way I experience You each Sabbath morning through the touch of your Holy Spirit.

FEBRUARY 1

I have learned that God answers prayers in three ways: "Yes;" "Not now;" and "No, I have something better for you." I need to remember that.

Compassionate God, I kneel before You and pray for friends and family who need You, whose burdens are too much to carry alone:
the ones whose struggle with temptation is a daily reality;
families whose conflicts have depleted their spirits;
caregivers who often love too much and suffer in quiet exhaustion;
each one who has faced the unspeakable and is now living with a grief painful beyond words.
In this moment of quiet, I offer to You the deepest prayers of my own heart.
Let your Spirit give consolation and healing and hope this day.

On the day *I needed You*, I called, and You responded
and infused my soul with strength.
Psalm 138:3 (The Voice)

Coyote, Yellowstone National Park, Wyoming

FEBRUARY 2

God of all generations, I often feel like Abraham starting his journey of faith into the unknown. This is a time in my life when I am anxious about not having control over the itinerary of my life, of not always being able to choose the route. Help me to surrender enough to let You lead me into the unknown, trusting your faithfulness. Overcome my fears with your love and my hesitancy with your plan for my wholeness. I pray that your peace might be the oasis in my wilderness so that I might truly experience renewal from
the prisons of old patterns to the hope of real change,
dead dreams to real possibilities,
and earth-bound knowledge to faith-centered wisdom.

Even when there was no reason for hope, Abraham kept hoping—believing that he would become the father of many nations. For God had said to him, "That's how many descendants you will have!" And Abraham's faith did not weaken, even though, at about 100 years of age, he figured his body was as good as dead—and so was Sarah's womb.
Abraham never wavered in believing God's promise. In fact, his faith grew stronger, and in this he brought glory to God. He was fully convinced that God is able to do whatever he promises. Romans 4:18-21 (NLT)

What do I need to surrender in this moment?

FEBRUARY 3

In this quiet moment, Precious Lord, I turn to You hoping to sense You speaking to me. I pray that You would re-center my life on what is important—your will and your ways, and what will matter beyond this day or this week. Why do I look for your presence in the flashy and forget that your voice doesn't shout at me over the din of my cluttered life? But then, in the silence that comes after I collapse in exhaustion, You surprise me. You seek me out and whisper your words of peace and acceptance. Then I let go and somehow quietly surrender to You. So reach out to me as I reach out to You this morning as I seek to connect with You—to listen.

I'm listening, Lord.

The LORD is near to all who call on him,
*   to all who call on him in truth.*
Psalm 145:18 (NIV)

What is most important today?

FEBRUARY 4

O God of wonders, You deserve my praise—all of earth abounds with glimpses of heaven's joy. Lost for a moment in the glory of a coral sunset or the diamond-studded midnight skies, I capture just a glimpse of your majesty and stand in awe. How wonderfully rich my life is with You!

Prepare me, O God, to be a sanctuary for You—with openness of spirit, sensitivity of heart, and strength of will to be one of your people in this world of need.

Yours, LORD, is the greatness and the power
*   and the glory and the majesty and the splendor,*
*   for everything in heaven and earth is yours.*
Yours, LORD, is the kingdom;
*   you are exalted as head over all.*
1 Chronicles 29:11 (NIV)

Naples, Florida

FEBRUARY 5

Blessed Lord, as I turn my heart to You in prayer today, grant me a brush of the Spirit in my heart, a catch in my breath, and space in my thoughts so that I might be yours in a new way, on a fresh journey with You. Grant me the desire to risk more than is comfortable, to give more than I think I can spare, to love more than I know how to love so that my life might reflect the secret joy of life in You.

This is my command: Love one another the way I loved you. This is the very best way to love. Put your life on the line for your friends. You are my friends when you do the things I command you. I'm no longer calling you servants because servants don't understand what their master is thinking and planning. No, I've named you friends because I've let you in on everything I've heard from the Father. John 15:12-15 (The Message)

Where do I sense God leading me on my journey?

FEBRUARY 6

O God of unsurpassing goodness, in the quiet of this time, I am still and bow my heart before You as I seek to enter more deeply into your presence. I know far too well the struggles and limitations I bring with me this morning. Yet, I come to You in trust that your love reaches out to me even in the midst of my failures. You pick me up, dust me off, and remind me that your love embraces me in the darkest experiences of life. Even when I wrestle with entering into silence to meet You, You seek me out and speak your words of grace in whatever stillness my mind can embrace. So I come here this morning to try to do just that—to connect with You, to trust your goodness, and to simply be open enough to receive.

Test yourselves to make sure you are solid in the faith. Don't drift along taking everything for granted. Give yourselves regular checkups. You need firsthand evidence, not mere hearsay, that Jesus Christ is in you. Test it out. If you fail the test, do something about it. I hope the test won't show that we have failed. But if it comes to that, we'd rather the test showed our failure than yours. We're rooting for the truth to win out in you. We couldn't possibly do otherwise.
We don't just put up with our limitations; we celebrate them, and then go on to celebrate every strength, every triumph of the truth in you. We pray hard that it will all come together in your lives. 2 Corinthians 13:5-9 (The Message)

I trust God to . . .

FEBRUARY 7

O Lord of all creation, for whom the mountains bow down and the valleys are exalted, I take this moment to worship You—with heart, mind, and spirit. In the midst of uncertainty and this time of waiting, I thank You for being here with me right now. I confess that waiting does not sit well with me, Lord. I like to be active as if I could somehow control life that way. Help me to live in this moment, trusting You to grant me the resources to live just this one day resting in You.

Blessed are those who listen to me,
watching daily at my doors,
waiting at my doorway.
For those who find me find life
and receive favor from the LORD.
Proverbs 8:34-35 (NIV)

Mt. Mansfield, Vermont

FEBRUARY 8

One of the truths I am realizing is that God's presence is never forced on my busy life. God always waits for my invitation.

O Lord, I am praying for many reasons today. Most of all, I long to feel a connection with You and with others. Yet, my lifestyle often keeps me so preoccupied, hurrying, producing, building and achieving, that I forget what is most important—You. Although my mind tells me that You are here with me, my spirit longs to feel your presence. Lord, where do I go from here? How do I slow down and find your presence in each moment? Teach me to abide in You throughout my day.

Hear this, Job.
   Pause *where you are*, and ponder the wonders of God.
Job 37:14 (The Voice)

How can I pause today to be more aware of God?

FEBRUARY 9

O God of tenderness, You offer me soul therapy when I come with an honest heart. Some of my prayers are for my own needs when I shoulder burdens beyond my ability to bear. Yet others are for those I know who need your presence:

> those who need a dose of determination;
> those facing decisions with limited choices;
> those who feel hemmed in by their helplessness;
> those whose waning hope begs for an infusion of encouragement.

Help me to let go, in complete trust that You will care for my concerns with a love far deeper than I can conceive or imagine. Enable me to release those concerns into your care trusting that your goodness will satisfy all my needs.

Now let your unfailing love comfort me,
* just as you promised me, your servant.*
Psalm 119:76 (NLT)

Lord, I give You my concerns for . . .

FEBRUARY 10

Gracious God, as I stop to ponder this past week, I am grateful for the moments when I have been privileged to discover You on the mountaintops of life. Thank you for those instants when I was able to sense the power of your presence in the most unexpected ways—when I saw a grandchild run into his grammy's arms at the airport, when I first glimpsed the turquoise-blue of a calm ocean, when a friend offered affirmation when I least expected it. Lord, thank you for all the joy bursts in my life.

. . . I came to give life with joy and abundance. John 10:10b (The Voice)

FEBRUARY 11

Heavenly Father, I dare to come into your presence because You have invited me to seek and to ask. I dare to come confessing my shortcomings because You are the God of second chances. I dare to come as your child because You have adopted me into your family. Through the power of your Holy Spirit, I ask that You would comfort me in my trials and stir me from my complacency so that my life might be a living memorial to your grace poured out for me through Jesus Christ, my Lord.

Even before he made the world, God loved us and chose us in Christ to be holy and without fault in his eyes. God decided in advance to adopt us into his own family by bringing us to himself through Jesus Christ. This is what he wanted to do, and it gave him great pleasure. Ephesians 1:4-5 (NLT)

I want a second chance to . . .

FEBRUARY 12

Loving Lord, even though I have known that You are the source of living water, I find myself searching for countless other temptations to fill my life—success, security, popularity, money, and pleasure. And in the end, each one is a dry well. Help me to remember that it is your love that fills my empty spaces and helps me to realize my significance in this world. Anything else will not satisfy.

As my thoughts center more and more on You, trust begins to displace my anxieties. And as my trust increases, I find myself strangely at peace in the circumstances that would have caused me anxiety before—the peace You promised that passes all understanding.

Soon a Samaritan woman came to draw water, and Jesus said to her, "Please give me a drink." He was alone at the time because his disciples had gone into the village to buy some food.

The woman was surprised, for Jews refuse to have anything to do with Samaritans. She said to Jesus, "You are a Jew, and I am a Samaritan woman. Why are you asking me for a drink?"

Jesus replied, "If you only knew the gift God has for you and who you are speaking to, you would ask me, and I would give you living water."

"But sir, you don't have a rope or a bucket," she said, "and this well is very deep. Where would you get this living water? And besides, do you think you're greater than our ancestor Jacob, who gave us this well? How can you offer better water than he and his sons and his animals enjoyed?"

Jesus replied, "Anyone who drinks this water will soon become thirsty again. But those who drink the water I give will never be thirsty again. It becomes a fresh, bubbling spring within them, giving them eternal life." John 4:7-14 (NLT)

Despite my temptations I can . . .

FEBRUARY 13

Dear Lord, I ask that You would kindle the flame of faith that burns deep within me, energizing me to do your will in your ways. O Lord, clear away any self-serving thoughts in my prayer today. I ask You to provide me with eternal perspective, helping me to discern the difference between waiting in a traffic jam and waiting for the results of a biopsy. Help me to surrender enough to let You lead me into the unknown, trusting your faithfulness.

Test me, LORD, and try me,
*   examine my heart and my mind;*
for I have always been mindful of your unfailing love
*   and have lived in reliance on your faithfulness.*
Psalm 26:2-3 (NIV)

Portland Head Light, Portland Maine

FEBRUARY 14

O Lord of my heart, thank you for the people in my life who are easy to love. Thank you for family and friends who understand me, who encourage me in my decisions, and whose presence can lift the burdens of difficult days. Create deep within me the unquenchable desire to love even the troublesome ones in my life. My prayer is that You would walk with me, sustain me, and teach me to use your all-encompassing love in every aspect of my life. I pray in the name of the one who has walked before me, Jesus Christ, my Lord.

If I speak in the tongues of men or of angels, but do not have love, I am only a resounding gong or a clanging cymbal. And if I have the gift of prophesy and can fathom all mysteries and all knowledge, and if I have a faith that can move mountains, but do not have love, I am nothing. If I give all I possess to the poor, and give over my body to hardship that I may boast, but do not have love, I gain nothing.
Love is patient, love is kind. It does not envy, it does not boast, it is not proud. It does not dishonor others, it is not self-seeking, it is not easily angered, it keeps no record of wrongs. Love does not delight in evil but rejoices with the truth. It always protects, always trusts, always hopes, always perseveres.
Love never fails . . . 1 Corinthians 13:1-8a (NIV)

Who are the ones I love who need God's touch?

FEBRUARY 15

One of my life lessons has been to learn, "The best I can do is not what I can do, but what God can do through me." (Anonymous)

Eternal God, as the time of Lenten reflection approaches, I seek to be transformed by You. Give me an honest and open heart so that I might be willing to
see my life through your eyes,
experience your love,
and take the next steps of faith to serve You and others.
Trusting your faithfulness, I pray in the name of my Lord, Jesus Christ.

Keep alert, stand firm in your faith, be courageous, be strong. Let all that you do be done in love. 1 Corinthians 16:13-14 (NRSV)

During Lent I want to reflect on . . .

FEBRUARY 16

Merciful God, You feed my spirit when I am hungry; You search for me when I am wandering without a way; and You strengthen me when I am beyond weariness. Whenever I am trudging through a path of uncertainty that blinds me to hope, through a dry spiritual desert that leaves me longing for an oasis of rest, I come in hope that You will once again speak to me in a way that I might know it is You—and help me to find the true center of my life.

O True God, You are my God, the *One whom I trust.*
   I seek You *with every fiber of my being.*
In this dry and weary land with no water in sight,
   my soul is dry and longs for You.
   My body aches for You, *for Your presence.*
Psalm 63:1 (The Voice)

Death Valley National Park, CA   Claire Beck

FEBRUARY 17

Thank you, Gentle Teacher, for revealing my carefully masked pride. Release me from the many ways that I construct a false self to those around me. Guard me from thinking more highly of myself than is merited; keep me from diminishing myself so that I am unable to become that person You envision me to be.

In my human frailty, I ask You to help me surrender my limitations to You, knowing that your power is made perfect in weakness and that your grace is more than I could ever need. For it is your grace and enduring compassion that lift me up, touch my heart, give peace to my soul, remodel my life, and teach me how to love.

But he said to me, "My grace is sufficient for you, for my power is made perfect in weakness." Therefore I will boast all the more gladly about my weaknesses, so that Christ's power may rest on me. 2 Corinthians 12:9 (NIV)

These are the weaknesses I offer to God . . .

FEBRUARY 18

Lord of the pilgrimage, at times I have chosen a path that leads me away from your presence. It might have been a slight detour, or it might have been a U-turn, but You call me to trust You enough to allow You to correct my course. Grant me the courage to say, "Lord, I release my control. I give it to You. I trust You to lead me back home to You."

(The Apostle Paul wrote) *It wasn't so long ago that you were mired in that old stagnant life of sin. You let the world, which doesn't know the first thing about living, tell you how to live. You filled your lungs with polluted unbelief, and then exhaled disobedience. We all did it, all of us doing what we felt like doing, when we felt like doing it, all of us in the same boat. It's a wonder God didn't lose his temper and do away with the whole lot of us. Instead, immense in mercy and with an incredible love, he embraced us. He took our sin-dead lives and made us alive in Christ. He did all this on his own, with no help from us! Then he picked us up and set us down in highest heaven in company with Jesus, our Messiah.*
Ephesians 2:1-6 (The Message)

Lord, I release control of . . .

FEBRUARY 19

Lord God, Creator of the universe, this winter day of splendor calls me into your presence, and I am truly amazed by the wonder of your creation. You spun the planets into orbit and the stars into being. You breathed the essence of life into all that exists and fashioned beauty into every corner of this earth. Yet, I often walk through life blind to all that You are. O Lord, help me to step away from the smallness of my vision to see the vastness of your glory as I seek to worship You.

Sing to him, sing praise to him;
*   tell of all his wonderful acts.*
Glory in his holy name;
*   let the hearts of those who seek the LORDrejoice.*
Look to the LORD and his strength;
*   seek his face always.*
1 Chronicles 16:9-11 (NIV)

Oregon

FEBRUARY 20

O Lord, I am thankful for the purpose and possibilities You have offered to me. Yet, I know I have often chosen to wander the path of fear rather than follow You in faith. I have been envious of what others have instead of rejoicing in your abundance. I have worried incessantly instead of surrendering to You in trust. Tender Shepherd, lead my heart back home to You this day.

Be Thou My Vision
No doubt about it! God is good —
*   good to good people, good to the good-hearted.*
But I nearly missed it,
*   missed seeing his goodness.*
I was looking the other way,
*   looking up to the people*
* At the top,*
*   envying the wicked who have it made,*
Who have nothing to worry about,
*   not a care in the whole wide world. . .*
When I was beleaguered and bitter,
*   totally consumed by envy,*
I was totally ignorant, a dumb ox
*   in your very presence.*
I'm still in your presence,
*   but you've taken my hand.*
You wisely and tenderly lead me,
*   and then you bless me.*
Psalm 73:1-5, 21-24 (The Message)

Today I can pursue my purpose in life by . . .

FEBRUARY 21

O Creator of this new day, I am grateful for those moments when I experience the incredible wonder of living—especially as the sunbursts of morning light wash over the horizon and melt away the last glimpses of darkness. In that morning stillness all of creation seems to stir, shake sleep away, and awaken to a fresh day of promise. It is in those seconds of grace-filled awe that I find myself amazed and grateful—and I am led back to You.

It is good to give thanks to the LORD,
  to sing praises to the Most High.
It is good to proclaim your unfailing love in the morning,
  your faithfulness in the evening,
accompanied by a ten-stringed instrument, a harp,
  and the melody of a lyre.
Psalm 92: 1-3 (NLT)

Thank you, Lord, for . . .

FEBRUARY 22

I remember reading one of Anne Lamott's insightful books and pausing to smile when she wrote, "Laughter is carbonated holiness."

Life-changing Lord, in mystery and miracle You are ever present, waiting for me to recognize your majesty all around me. Thank you for music that melts my defenses and ushers me into your presence, for laughter that frees me from taking myself too seriously, for the stillness of an evening resting with those I love. I am thankful for the littlest ones who greet each day with wonder and the oldest ones whose lives offer us so much wisdom.

How amazing are the deeds of the LORD!
All who delight in him should ponder them . . .
Fear of the LORD is the foundation of true wisdom.
All who obey his commandments will grow in wisdom.
Praise him forever!
Psalm 111:2,10 (NLT)

Bhutan

FEBRUARY 23

O God of the ages and God of this moment in time, I have sensed You drawing me closer. Your presence may be like a meteor shower in the midst of a dark night, or sometimes much more subtle, like a small awareness that opens my mind and spirit to growth in You. Much like the first disciples, when I have chosen to take the risk to respond, You have answered. You reassure me that I am deeply cherished in a world that often shouts that I am not enough. You have given me the courage to risk more than I might have attempted without your strength. I have even dared to make a difference in someone else's life with a strength that I know is not my own, but yours.

Your unfailing love, O LORD, is as vast as the heavens;
  your faithfulness reaches beyond the clouds.
Psalm 36:5 (NLT)

How can I make a difference today?

FEBRUARY 24

Blessed Savior, I turn to You, trusting that your grace is sufficient for my needs. Thank you for my community of faith that upholds me, granting comfort and joy. I pray for those who were blessed with good news this week and those who heard difficult words. As I linger in the quiet, You bring to mind the concerns I have shouldered all week for the special people You have entrusted to me: the ones who have lost their way but are discovering new directions; the ones who are dogged by discouragement and for whom hope is only a word; and the ones so stuck in a situation that a positive outcome seems only wishful thinking.

O God, You are the Lord of impossibilities, the Author of new beginnings, the Architect of hope-filled futures. I ask You to step in and be at work in each and every situation I entrust to You this brand new day.

But you, O LORD, are a shield around me;
*   you are my glory, the one who holds my head high.*
I cried out to the LORD,
and he answered me from his holy mountain.
I lay down and slept,
*   yet I woke up in safety,*
*   for the LORD was watching over me.*
Psalm 3:3-5 (NLT)

Lord, please help me to . . .

FEBRUARY 25

Precious Lord, You have called me by name and claimed me as your own. Yet I am so aware that I have kept back much of myself from You—holding back from the complete renewal You desire for me. I haven't begun to do what You could do through me if I would only step out in faith. Release me from my fears and plant in me the desire to live my life with meaning and purpose in your kingdom. And then empower me to do far more than I could ever ask or imagine in your name.

I'm baptizing you here in the river, turning your old life in for a kingdom life. The real action comes next: The main character in this drama—compared to him I'm a mere stagehand—will ignite the kingdom life within you, a fire within you, the Holy Spirit within you, changing you from the inside out. He's going to clean house—make a clean sweep of your lives. He'll place everything true in its proper place before God; everything false he'll put out with the trash to be burned. Matthew 3:11-12 (The Message)

Barred owl, Vermont

FEBRUARY 26

Lord, my Counselor, as I center on You, I seek to be honest with You and with myself. I have tucked away some painful fragments shrouded in hidden compartments of my mind that I ask You to bring to light—the hurts, resentments, and bitterness to which I secretly cling. I rehash and rehearse them until they are as comfortable as an old blanket. Yet deep within me, I know differently; they are leaching joy and purpose from my life in You. As I release them, I ask that You would do a thorough house cleaning, clearing out anything that has become an obstacle in my relationships with You or with other people.

"These words I speak to you are not incidental additions to your life, homeowner improvements to your standard of living. They are foundational words, words to build a life on. If you work these words into your life, you are like a smart carpenter who built his house on solid rock. Rain poured down, the river flooded, a tornado hit—but nothing moved that house. It was fixed to the rock.
"But if you just use my words in Bible studies and don't work them into your life, you are like a stupid carpenter who built his house on the sandy beach. When a storm rolled in and the waves came up, it collapsed like a house of cards."
When Jesus concluded his address, the crowd burst into applause. They had never heard teaching like this. It was apparent that he was living everything he was saying—quite a contrast to their religion teachers! This was the best teaching they had ever heard. Matthew 7:24-29 (The Message)

If I let go of my obstacles, I could . . .

FEBRUARY 27

Abba God, throughout my prayer time I seek to still myself—quiet myself—and to respond to the flow of your Holy Spirit. Yet sometimes my own rambling thoughts completely distract me. Then I ask that You would center me and break through my defenses to truly change me. Yahweh, I know that I am richly blessed because You have reminded me that

I didn't choose You, Lord. You chose me;

I know You because You first knew me;

I love You because You first loved me.

Grant me the desire to live deeply by the power of your Spirit within me, so that You might give me the strength I need to journey ever deeper into the way of Jesus, my Lord.

The one who follows His teaching and walks this path lives in an intimate relationship with God. How do we know that He lives in us? By the gift of His Spirit. 1 John 3:24 (The Voice)

I know your Holy Spirit lives within me because . . .

FEBRUARY 28

O God of all life, I offer You my grateful praise for all the blessings You so abundantly give to me:

seagulls soaring into the heavens,

a fragrant cup of coffee that welcomes a new morning,

the deep delight that overflows when I think of the ones I love,

and all the ways I see You at work in my life.

For all the gifts You grant to me that are easy to see and for those You give that are disguised, for the blessings I recognize, and for those I fail to notice—for each one, O Lord, hear my prayers of gratitude.

I said to myself, "Relax and rest.
   GOD has showered you with blessings."
Psalm 116:7 (The Message)

Stonington, Maine

FEBRUARY 29

As I seek your will, Lord, give me enough vision to seek the next step along the path You have prepared for me. When fear keeps me from taking risks of faith, grant me the courage to move forward anyway. So often I am trapped by anxiety over what the future holds. Remind me to abide in You, trusting in your goodness and empowered by your strength. O Lord, You are the ever-open door. You opened yourself to accept me, even before I knew I was seeking You. Take away the roadblocks in me so that I might be willing to become the person You created me to be. Help me to be open to that inner encouraging voice, reminding me that You have created me to be restless until I somehow find my rest in You.

The LORD is my light and my salvation —
*   whom shall I fear?*
The LORD is the stronghold of my life —
*   of whom shall I be afraid?*
Psalm 27:1 (NIV)

What roadblocks prevent me from becoming the person God intended me to be?

Be Thou My Vision

Be thou my vision, O Lord of my heart,
Be all else but naught to me, save that thou art;
Thou my best thought in the day and the night,
Both waking and sleeping, thy presence my light.
Be thou my wisdom, be thou my true word,
Be thou ever with me, and I with thee Lord;
Be thou my great Father, and I thy true son;
Be thou in me dwelling, and I with thee one.
Be thou my breastplate, my sword for the fight;
Be thou my whole armour, be thou my true might;
Be thou my soul's shelter, be thou my strong tower:
O raise thou me heavenward, great Power of my power.
Riches I heed not, nor man's empty praise:
Be thou mine inheritance now and always;
Be thou and thou only the first in my heart;
O Sovereign of Heaven, my treasure thou art.
High King of Heaven, thou Heaven's bright sun,
O grant me its joys after victory is won!;
Great heart of my own heart, whatever befall,
Still be thou my vision, O Ruler of all.
Traditional Irish hymn, English version by Eleanor Hull, 1912

MARCH 1

Ever-renewing God, I give thanks for the promise of springtime in the air. On this day of sparkling sunshine, I find myself enlivened by the delights of creation. I pause for just a moment to enjoy the serenity of a walk on the beach, to drink in the waters of your grace, to absorb the wonders of your mercy, and to bow in worship to the One who provides it all.

This is the day that the LORD has made:
  let us rejoice and be glad in it.
Psalm 118:24 (NRSV)

Maine coast

MARCH 2

As we enter into this Lenten journey before Easter, I am reminded of the little saying that if I do the connecting, God will do the perfecting.

O Christ of the ages, your footsteps track the world, and your Spirit leans close to each whose heart invites your presence. It's an amazing thought to consider how much your love embraces me. And so I give myself to You. With my hands and heart and voice, I give back my life to You, whispering, "Here I am, Lord. Use me."

Then I heard the voice of the LORD saying, "Whom shall I send? And who will go for us?" And I said, "Here am I. Send me!" Isaiah 6:8 (NIV)

Here I am, Lord. Send me to . . .

MARCH 3

O Spirit of calm courage, I invite You to enter the deepest places in my heart to do the work of deep change, to root out my hidden sins, and to free me from any obstacles I place in my relationship with You or others. O Lord, let each one of my stumbling blocks become stepping-stones to a deeper connection with You. Help me to dare boldly in You, open to wherever You lead me. Help me to trust deeply in your power at work in my life.

True wisdom and real power belong to God;
  from him we learn how to live,
  and also what to live for.
Job 12:13 (The Message)

My stumbling blocks are . . .

MARCH 4

Loving Lord, as the seasons are made for change, so too is my life made for transition. Some changes I welcome as answers to prayer. Yet, other transitions bring with them a sense of trepidation. In these times, when my ordered life seems to collapse all around me, when I feel unmoored and alone, I am comforted in remembering your power stilling the wind and the waves on the Sea of Galilee. In this time of prayer, grant me the gift of a calmed spirit and a peaceful heart.

Then Jesus got into the boat and started across the lake with his disciples. Suddenly, a fierce storm struck the lake, with waves breaking into the boat. But Jesus was sleeping. The disciples went and woke him up, shouting, "Lord, save us! We're going to drown!"
Jesus responded, "Why are you afraid? You have so little faith!" Then he got up and rebuked the wind and waves, and suddenly there was a great calm.
The disciples were amazed. "Who is this man?" they asked. "Even the winds and waves obey him!" Matthew 8:23-27 (NLT)

Sea of Galilee, Israel   Tisa Queen-Oldham   71

MARCH 5

O Prince of Peace, in the anticipation of resting in your presence, I lift to You now what is stirring in my heart. Some are prayers for friends or family dealing with illness or loss. Some are prayers of concern for situations that stress my spirit. Some are prayers for the troubles swirling around in our world—situations of fear or injustice or hatred that cry out for your healing. In times when it is difficult to be hopeful, remind me that You always provide a way where there seems to be no way.

God is our refuge and strength,
  an ever-present help in trouble.
Therefore we will not fear, though the earth give way
  and the mountains fall into the heart of the sea,
though its waters roar and foam
  and the mountains quake with their surging.
Psalm 46:1-3 (NIV)

Today my prayers for others include . . .

MARCH 6

Blessed Savior, teach me to wait with You day by day in quiet ways as I invite the power of your Spirit to change my life into an instrument of your grace. Teach me to see with new eyes the wonders that exist all around me. Take away my weariness, my blindness to what is beautiful and sacred. Increase my sensitivity to the people and situations around me so that You might use my gifts to be a blessing to each person.

So, chosen by God for this new life of love, dress in the wardrobe God picked out for you: compassion, kindness, humility, quiet strength, discipline. Be even-tempered, content with second place, quick to forgive an offense. Forgive as quickly and completely as the Master forgave you. And regardless of what else you put on, wear love. It's your basic, all-purpose garment. Never be without it. Colossians 3:12-14 (The Message)

Help me to be sensitive to . . .

Tropicbird, Ecuador

Jeff Wendorff

MARCH 7

Merciful God, I sense that I am in the midst of a wintering season in my life. I am like a tree whose leaves have fallen, waiting for spring's new blossoms of life to appear. My empty heart is waiting, sometimes patiently, oftentimes not, for your presence to break through in ways I can see:

    resentments released,

        a freedom promised,

            direction revealed,

                a prayer answered,

                    spirit renewed.

O God, I want to live my life in such a way that I not only turn to You in the crises of my life, but also walk with You in the calmer, joyful days. Take me by the hand, remind me again to leave my burdens in the arms of your Son, Jesus Christ, and lead me into a deeper faith and a fuller discipleship so that I might soar again on the wings of your freedom.

Have you not known? Have you not heard?
The LORD is the everlasting God,
   the Creator of the ends of the earth.
He does not faint or grow weary;
   his understanding is unsearchable.
He gives power to the faint,
   and strengthens the powerless.
Even youths will faint and be weary,
   And the young will fall exhausted;
but those who wait for the LORD shall renew their strength,
   they will mount up with wings like eagles;
they shall run and not be weary,
   they shall walk and not faint.
Isaiah 40:28-31 (NRSV)

MARCH 8

O Lord of the quiet whisper, You are waiting for me, inviting me to turn to You, but far too often I am too busy. I confess that this quiet is often very difficult for me. I prefer to be surrounded by activity and noise and distraction. Sometimes, silence unsettles me and reflection rattles me. So I seek diversions and welcome interruptions. I fill my schedule to overflowing. And yet, deep within me, a hunger grows and grows. A hunger for silence. A hunger for solitude. A hunger for reflection. A hunger for You, O God. And the busier I get, the more this hunger grows. When I finally quiet the busy monster, I settle in and discover that You have been with me all along. Help me to take a step to seek You this day. Drive away the fears that make me shrink back from silence. Teach me how to be still and know You. Then refill me by the power of your Holy Spirit with a faith vibrant and full so that others might see abundant life—and in so doing discover the One who is the source of all life, Jesus Christ, my Lord.

For God alone, O my soul, wait in silence,
*   for my hope is from him.*
Psalm 62:5 English Standard Version (ESV)

In my life I seem to be easily distracted by . . .

MARCH 9

O God of light, during this Lenten season of returning to You, I dare to open my whole self to your converting work of love. Yet, I have also discovered the many hurdles that I often place in the way. I recognize how often I rest in denial and resist seeing the truth about my behaviors; how attached I become to being right; how I cannot bear to have my less-than-perfect self shown; how I succumb to fears and shrink from risking. Yet, You see me as my perfectly imperfect self and love me just the same. In the cross of Christ, You have loved me extravagantly, even when I have loved little in return. And yet, You continue to invite me to come to You, to trust You, to surrender myself into your care. You are indeed an awesome God.

This is the message we heard from Jesus and now declare to you: God is light, and there is no darkness in him at all. So we are lying if we say we have fellowship with God but go on living in spiritual darkness; we are not practicing the truth. But if we are living in the light, as God is in the light, then we have fellowship with each other, and the blood of Jesus, his Son, cleanses us from all sin. If we claim we have no sin, we are only fooling ourselves and not living in the truth. But if we confess our sins to him, he is faithful and just to forgive us our sins and to cleanse us from all wickedness. 1 John 1:5-9 (NLT)

When I examine my vulnerabilities before God, I . . .

MARCH 10

Gracious God, I offer You my thanksgiving for all the blessings You so abundantly give to me—eagles rising on the wind, flower petals trembling in the invisible breeze, the complex mysteries of healing within a human cell, and the comfort of a genuine smile on a gloomy day. As I contemplate your wonders, help me to be inspired so that I might be

a little more aware,

a little more caring,

a little more compassionate,

a little more like Jesus.

And now, just as you accepted Christ Jesus as your Lord, you must continue to follow him. Let your roots grow down into him, and let your lives be built on him. Then your faith will grow strong in the truth you were taught, and you will overflow with thankfulness. Colossians 2:6-7 (NLT)

Hepatica, Vermont

MARCH 11

Too often in my life I talk trust, but I live worry. When I do that, one of the most centering remedies I can do is breathe in the Holy Spirit and breathe out worry.

Compassionate Lord, help me to cope with the many concerns on my mind—some for my own needs and some for others' burdens. Look beneath my smile and see the needs that I bring. Help me to be courageous enough to bring my whole self to You. It is my prayer, O Lord, that You would
    light a new fire in the lukewarm ashes of my faith,
    give a new peace to my worried, weary heart,
    and help me to embrace new beginnings.
May your grace be sufficient for each and every day as I trust You to guide my ways, through Jesus Christ.

This is my command—be strong and courageous! Do not be afraid or discouraged. For the LORD your God is with you wherever you go.
Joshua 1:9 (NLT)

Today I feel anxious about . . .

MARCH 12

Lord Jesus, teach me to pray. As I draw near to You in thought, my spirit longs for the reach of your grace, but I simply do not know how to express the deepest concerns that lie hidden in my heart. I am grateful for the sense of need that keeps me close to your side. Help me to keep my hand in yours and my ears open to the wisdom of your voice.

And the Holy Spirit helps us in our weakness. For example, we don't know what God wants us to pray for. But the Holy Spirit prays for us with groanings that cannot be expressed in words. And the Father who knows all hearts knows what the Spirit is saying, for the Spirit pleads for us believers in harmony with God's own will. Romans 8:26-27 (NLT)

What needs do I offer to God today?

MARCH 13

Dear Lord, today I remember my friends and family with thankfulness, for they have touched my spirit, leaving the mark of their love. Some have gifted me with laughter that has transcended the difficulties of the hour. Some have shared life stories that have enabled me to grow in wisdom. Some have made me feel needed and appreciated. So, lead me to offer those same gifts to those I know—to bring peace where there is anxiety, to bring assurance where there is fear, to offer a glimmer of hope where there is none, all in the name of the One who is my strength and my peace, Jesus Christ, my Lord.

Whatever is good and perfect is a gift coming down to us from God our Father, who created all the lights in the heavens. He never changes or casts a shifting shadow. James 1:17 (NLT)

MARCH 14

Caring and compassionate God, I pray for each person who feels helpless before the obstacles that surround them. I pray for those who are holding on to creeping resentments, for I know that being unable to forgive destroys not only others but myself as well. Thank you, Lord, for all these challenges of life that have made me count on your sustaining grace—for the failures that have made me wiser, for the trials that have made me stronger, and for the disappointments that, in the end, have helped me turn to You. I know that I am never alone and that I can always trust You.

Then Peter came to him and asked, "Lord, how often should I forgive someone who sins against me? Seven times?"
"No, not seven times," Jesus replied, "but seventy times seven!
Matthew 18:21-22 (NLT)

Today I need to forgive . . .

MARCH 15

O Living Lord, in this Lenten season, I invite You to lead me on the path toward integrity of soul. I take just a moment before You to reflect on all the things that I allow to influence me—either for good or for ill. Some of those influences lift me up, encouraging me to dream more deeply, to serve more enthusiastically, and to seek You more faithfully. Yet, as I face You with an honest heart, I also have to confess that some things I allow into my life bring out the worst version of myself:

   when I allow other people's opinions to matter too much,

   when I listen to voices telling me to seek one more possession to be happier,

   and when I pursue what I want no matter the cost to someone else.

You promise that when I confess my shortcomings, You are faithful and just and will forgive me and set me on the path of life again.

Create in me a pure heart, O God,
   and renew a steadfast spirit within me.
Do not cast me from your presence
   or take your Holy Spirit from me.
Restore to me the joy of your salvation
   and grant me a willing spirit, to sustain me.
Psalm 51:10-12 (NIV)

Give me a willing spirit to . . .

MARCH 16

Abba God, I thank you for the potential You see in each of your children. Lord, I can be so much more. Even when I have failed or lost my way, I trust You can do anything with my life. With You nothing is impossible; with You no door is closed to me. My life can go as far as I will let You take it.

(The Apostle Paul wrote) *I'm not saying that I have this all together, that I have it made. But I am well on my way, reaching out for Christ, who has so wondrously reached out for me. Friends, don't get me wrong: By no means do I count myself an expert in all of this, but I've got my eye on the goal, where God is beckoning us onward—to Jesus. I'm off and running, and I'm not turning back.* Philippians 3:12-14 (The Message)

Outer Banks, North Carolina

MARCH 17

As the disciples sat at Jesus' feet, they learned how to live a life fully in You, O God, reaching out to You in prayer. Yet, during this season of Lent, I come before You today fighting so many different feelings. Part of me couldn't wait to begin this time of prayer; part of me barely made it out of bed. I confess I face too many prayerless times when my weary emptiness becomes a burden because I have nothing left to give. Sometimes I know exactly why I pray; other times I'm not so sure. Still, something calls me to You, so I have come to seek You and to pray in grateful surrender.

Nevertheless, listen to my prayer and my plea, O LORD my God. Hear the cry and the prayer that your servant is making to you today. 1 Kings 8:28 (NLT)

I am too busy with . . .

MARCH 18

O God of abundant life, in this time of prayer I turn to You hoping to sense You speaking words of love and forgiveness, of grace and peace. I know You love me as I am, but with vast patience and mercy You are ever-changing me. Help me to re-orient my priorities so that I might more fully live my life with purpose and meaning and see the opportunities to serve You as daily gifts.

While Jesus was living in the Galilean hills, John, called "the Baptizer," was preaching in the desert country of Judea. His message was simple and austere, like his desert surroundings: "Change your life. God's kingdom is here." Matthew 3:1 (The Message)

What would I like to change?

MARCH 19

Finding a way to be grateful is at the heart of my spiritual life. Whether I am enjoying a gentle breeze or facing the storms that are raging around me, if I can find my way back to gratitude, I know I am centered on the Lord.

Yahweh, God of all creation, your glory is echoed in the fanfare of melodies filling the earth—where each new day dawns to awaken the world, where your mighty power blows the breeze of spring, and where awakening landscapes blossom into life. I see the miracle of your mighty works in the world and simply marvel. I praise your name and whisper, "Amen."

May the glory of the LORD endure forever;
   may the LORD rejoice in his works,
Psalm 104:31 (ESV)

Gold Beach, Redwood National Park, CA

MARCH 20

Eternal One, so often I want to believe that my faith would ensure security from all harm, that to trust in You is to be insulated from the harsh realities of living, and that to be faithful is to be guaranteed the blessings of life. I confess that these are the wishful myths of my faith. In my more honest moments, I recognize that it is in the struggles of living that I am most open to your grace. Pain is often the precursor to healing; despair is often the pathway to hope; death gives birth to everlasting life. In my weakness, I experience your strength most powerfully. Lord, take my prayers, sifting them so that You might work within me and change me to become more like my Savior, Jesus Christ.

"My thoughts are nothing like your thoughts," says the LORD.
"And my ways are far beyond anything you could imagine.
For just as the heavens are higher than the earth,
so my ways are higher than your ways
and my thoughts higher than your thoughts."
Isaiah 55:8-9 (NLT)

The challenges looming before me are . . .

MARCH 21

God of all generations, today I lift up the children and youth as many of them prepare to take the step of faith in affirming their faith in Christ. I pray that each one might hear You call them by name, reminding them that they are yours today and every day. Capture each of their hearts with a glimpse of what life lived with your passion and purpose might look like. I pray that You will pour out your Spirit upon them, helping them to grow in deepening wisdom and in daring courage so that You might use their willing hearts to make a difference for You in their worlds. O Lord, I pray that their example might inspire me to take risks of faith in my life, trusting You with the outcome.

When I think of all this, I fall to my knees and pray to the Father, the Creator of everything in heaven and on earth. I pray that from his glorious, unlimited resources he will empower you with inner strength through his Spirit. Then Christ will make his home in your hearts as you trust in him. Your roots will grow down into God's love and keep you strong. And may you have the power to understand, as all God's people should, how wide, how long, how high, and how deep his love is. May you experience the love of Christ, though it is too great to understand fully. Then you will be made complete with all the fullness of life and power that comes from God. Ephesians 3:14-19 (NLT)

Today I pray for the youth and children in my life . . .

MARCH 22

Ever-present Lord, I live in a world of cell phones, texts, and breaking news. The pace of my life often leaves me unsettled, sensing that there is more to this life, but unsure how to find it. So I come to this sanctuary of prayer, a place where I take time to sit down, to slow down, to breathe, to await the gift of your presence, and to drink deeply of your living water. And when I stop, I discover that I have raced by a thousand miracles that You have placed right before me. O God, when I stop and rest, I know that You offer a different way of living, one that begins with resting in You and trusting your love to sustain all of my life. For this opportunity to stop and breathe in your Holy Spirit, and be refreshed and renewed, I am thankful, Lord. Help me to live in this moment, trusting You to grant me the resources to live just this one day without the need to rush about.

But the Helper, the Holy Spirit, whom the Father will send in my name, he will teach you all things and bring to your remembrance all that I have said to you. John 14:26 (ESV)

Danby, Vermont

One of the pitfalls that I find to be true in my own life is my propensity to spend my time either rehashing the past or rehearsing the future. Have you ever noticed how exquisite life really is when you notice what God is up to in this moment? That's why some call it the "Sacrament of the Present Moment."

Precious Lord, take my hand and teach me the secret of living just one day at a time, knowing that each new day brings with it so much joy that I cannot fully explore it, so many blessings that I cannot even count them, and an eternal hope that comes from trusting You. Help me to practice "the Sacrament of the Present Moment" today and every day, in the name of the One who can do all things for those who live in Him, Jesus Christ, my Lord.

But blessed are those who trust in the LORD
*   and have made the LORD their hope and confidence.*
They are like trees planted along a riverbank,
*   with roots that reach deep into the water.*
Such trees are not bothered by the heat
*   or worried by long months of drought.*
Their leaves stay green,
*   and they never stop producing fruit.*
Jeremiah 17:7-8 (NLT)

In this moment I sense that . . .

MARCH 24

Life-changing Lord. as I rest in your holy presence, I come with an open and willing heart, ready to allow You to see the whole of my being—all my hopes, my dreams, my joys and my plans. But I also carry my failures, my struggles, my disappointments, and my pain. I have discovered that when I surrender and trust You, You begin the work of making me whole and prepare me again to live the life You have always envisioned for me.

I will give them a heart to know me, that I am the LORD. They will be my people, and I will be their God, for they will return to me with all their heart. Jeremiah 24:7 (NIV)

Make me whole so that I can . . .

MARCH 25

O God of wonders, on this Palm Sunday morning I am filled with joy, ready to praise You. As I anticipate the celebration of Easter, I ponder all the ways You have been at work in my life, the moments of laughter lightening the yoke of weariness, and the joyful explosion of melody that stirs my spirit. You have brought me here this morning to prepare my heart for the message of your love poured out in Jesus Christ.

As I remember the events of Holy Week, at times I have found myself, like the disciples, overwhelmed by the choices I have been offered and by the fears that have overtaken me. I know that I, too, might welcome You with palms one day and shout for your crucifixion the next. Lead me to the garden of prayer so that I might let go of anything that keeps me from You so that I might know your will and be given the courage to do it.

Shout to the LORD, all the earth;
*   break out in praise and sing for joy!*
Sing your praise to the LORD with the harp,
*   with the harp and melodious song,*
with trumpets and the sound of the ram's horn.
*   Make a joyful symphony before the LORD, the King!*
Psalm 98: 4-6 (NLT)

Coral Gables, Florida

MARCH 26

Holy Spirit, breathe your life into my singing, my praying, my speaking, my listening, my touching so that each might become a means of experiencing your presence. As I seek your will, give me clarity to understand your ways. When fear keeps me from taking steps of faith, grant me the courage to move forward anyway. So often I am caged by anxiety over what might or might not happen. Remind me to abide in You, trusting and resting in your goodness, empowered by your strength deep within me, through Jesus Christ, my Lord.

Humble yourselves therefore under the mighty hand of God, so that he may exalt you in due time. Cast all your anxiety on him, because he cares for you. Discipline yourselves, keep alert. Like a roaring lion your adversary the devil prowls around, looking for someone to devour. Resist him, steadfast in your faith, for you know that your brothers and sisters in all the world are undergoing the same kinds of suffering. And after you have suffered for a little while, the God of all grace, who has called you to his eternal glory in Christ, will himself restore, support, strengthen, and establish you. 1 Peter 5:6-10 (NRSV)

Lord, give me the courage to . . .

MARCH 27

Lord Jesus Christ, your welcome embraces me, inviting me to come close to find your touch upon my life. Help me to be humble enough to know that I need You. Open my eyes to the people You want me to serve—loved ones who need my attention, strangers to whom I can be a blessing, needs that I have the resources to meet. Wherever I go, let me be your hands, your feet, your laughter, your joy in your name.

Before the Passover celebration, Jesus knew that his hour had come to leave this world and return to his Father. He had loved his disciples during his ministry on earth, and now he loved them to the very end. It was time for supper, and the devil had already prompted Judas, son of Simon Iscariot, to betray Jesus. Jesus knew that the Father had given him authority over everything and that he had come from God and would return to God. So he got up from the table, took off his robe, wrapped a towel around his waist, and poured water into a basin. Then he began to wash the disciples' feet, drying them with the towel he had around him. John 13:1-5 (NLT)

I could be a blessing to . . .

MARCH 28

Almighty God, Maker of heaven and earth, the bounties of your blessings surround me. You reach out your hand until all of life bursts with showering colors and sounds of joy—from the melody of the morning bird calls, the fragrance of jasmine in full bloom, and the salty scent of the ocean breeze. The beauty lifts my spirit on soaring wings to glorify You. Together all of creation breathes in your Spirit and then breathes out one great hallelujah.

O my soul, bless GOD!
GOD, my God, how great you are!
* beautifully, gloriously robed,*
Dressed up in sunshine,
* and all heaven stretched out for your tent.*
You built your palace on the ocean deeps,
* made a chariot out of clouds and took off on wind-wings.*
You commandeered winds as messengers,
* appointed fire and flame as ambassadors.*
You set earth on a firm foundation
* so that nothing can shake it, ever.*
Psalm 104:1-5 (The Message)

Anguilla

MARCH 29

O God, whose presence is like a fountain of fresh water springing from a desert place, I come to You to drink deeply of your mercy. Yet, I think of the disciples, recognizing in them my own fear and weakness—and wavering. O Lord, even when I have denied or betrayed You, You have continued to reach out to me, calling me to come home to You. It is there that I find your compassionate eyes welcoming me as your beloved child. Enable me to face the truth about both my gifts and my failings so that I might stand firmly planted—not only in the power of the cross but also in the triumph of the resurrection.

About an hour later someone else insisted, "This must be one of them, because he is a Galilean, too."
But Peter said, "Man, I don't know what you are talking about." And immediately, while he was still speaking, the rooster crowed.
At that moment the Lord turned and looked at Peter. Suddenly, the Lord's words flashed through Peter's mind: "Before the rooster crows tomorrow morning, you will deny three times that you even know me." And Peter left the courtyard, weeping bitterly. Luke 22:59-62 (NLT)

Where has God called me to stand firm?

MARCH 30

Almighty God, I remember the night in which your Son left the comfort of an upper room and the safety of friends to enter the darkness—until You conquered the shadows on Easter morning. Your Son, Jesus the Christ, laid down his life to give the freedom of forgiveness, the gift of the Holy Spirit, and the promise of eternal life. Take away the fears that so entangle me; listen to the unspoken needs that live deeply within me. Help me to release all that I grasp too tightly. And then, grant me the grace to experience your presence so intimately that I might also trust your will, for I pray boldly in the name of my Lord, Jesus Christ.

Because of God's tender mercy,
*   the morning light from heaven is about to break upon us,*
to give light to those who sit in darkness and in the shadow of death,
*   and to guide us to the path of peace.*
Luke 1:78-79 (NLT)

Through God's grace I can . . .

MARCH 31

Emmanuel, God with me, I hold some thoughts so deeply in a hidden place of my soul that You alone know what resides there. You look deep within me and find beauty that even I fail to recognize. But my wounds need your healing, my habits and attitudes need your kind realignment, and my priorities need your steady encouragement. Lord, help me to be still enough to hear your whispers in my heart, and then grant me the strength to follow your guidance.

Teach me to do your will,
  for you are my God.
May your gracious Spirit lead me forward
  on a firm footing.
Psalm 143:10 (NLT)

Vermont

APRIL 1

Easter proclaims you can put love in a grave, but you can't keep it there.
(Anonymous)

O God of this vibrant Easter season, the earth blooms in celebration of
the resurrection of my Lord. In the bold hydrangeas and the trumpeting
lilies, I see that the earth remembers the morning after, when darkness was
replaced by a dawn unlike any other seen before. Despair was replaced by
unbridled joy; defeat, by ultimate victory; death, by a blast of a sealed stone
that couldn't contain the power of your love. So then, lift my spirit in song
and shelter my heart in prayer as I, too, join the celebration.

*After the Sabbath, at dawn on the first day of the week, Mary Magdalene and
the other Mary went to look at the tomb.*
*There was a violent earthquake, for an angel of the Lord came down from heaven
and, going to the tomb, rolled back the stone and sat on it. His appearance was
like lightning, and his clothes were white as snow. The guards were so afraid of
him that they shook and became like dead men.*
*The angel said to the women, "Do not be afraid, for I know that you are looking
for Jesus, who was crucified. He is not here; he has risen, just as he said. Come
and see the place where he lay. Then go quickly and tell his disciples: 'He has
risen from the dead and is going ahead of you into Galilee. There you will see
him.' Now I have told you."* Matthew 28:1-7 (NIV)

APRIL 2

O thank you, Lord, for the dawn of the magnificence of this Easter season. Thank you for the joy of worship, the beauty of your creation, the bright hue of springtime flowers, the trembling of the trees, the sun escaping through the clouds, and an expanse of windows that let in the morning glory.

I offer special gratitude for the gift of children, who remind me that your blessings are new every morning. Thank you for opening my eyes to your presence and helping me to recognize You in my world.

One day some parents brought their children to Jesus so he could lay his hands on them and pray for them. But the disciples scolded the parents for bothering him.

But Jesus said, "Let the children come to me. Don't stop them! For the Kingdom of Heaven belongs to those who are like these children." And he placed his hands on their heads and blessed them before he left.

Matthew 19:13-14 (NLT)

Children remind me that . . .

APRIL 3

God of glory, You meet me here where I recognize again the grace You so freely have given to me in Jesus Christ. I come into your presence with awe, for You are the One who imagined the brilliant flame of shooting stars and the purpled sky to close my day. But my heart fills with humble gratitude when I remember the sacrifice of love You offered in Jesus. I am so grateful that your love includes me, especially when I feel unworthy of that grace.

God saved you by his grace when you believed. And you can't take credit for this; it is a gift from God. Salvation is not a reward for the good things we have done, so none of us can boast about it. Ephesians 2:8-9 (NLT)

God's grace has given me . . .

APRIL 4

Wonderful, amazing God, I thank You for the gift of the resurrection, bringing me the promise of forgiveness and new life. With the dawning of this day, awaken me to new opportunities to love You and serve your people. Empower me as I use my life and my gifts to your glory. Allow me to know the deep joy of seeing lives touched because of what I have been able to contribute to the people I encounter, following in the path of Jesus.

Jesus told her, "I am the resurrection and the life. Anyone who believes in me will live, even after dying. John 11:25 (NLT)

Versailles, Kentucky

APRIL 5

O Risen Lord, awaken in me the fresh breeze of faith. Like the disciples, I walk to the tomb expecting nothing, and then You surprise me with your extravagant love. Roll aside any stones in my life, leaving the path to abundant life full of hope and open wide. I pray for the strength to stand for what is good and to live a life of integrity and peace so that I might be a fitting messenger of your love.

Now the eleven disciples went to Galilee, to the mountain to which Jesus had directed them. And when they saw him they worshiped him, but some doubted. And Jesus came and said to them, "All authority in heaven and on earth has been given to me. Go therefore and make disciples of all nations, baptizing them in the name of the Father and of the Son and of the Holy Spirit, teaching them to observe all that I have commanded you. And behold, I am with you always, to the end of the age." Matthew 28: 16-20 (ESV)

I have been surprised by Jesus' presence in . . .

APRIL 6

Lord of the journey, I do understand that the path to believing often travels through a place of doubting, and that understanding your ways sometimes means accepting without knowing. Take me to a place where I can learn to trust your heart, even when I cannot trace your hand. For You know and I know that at times, I simply cannot comprehend your ways. Out of my confusion, gentle Lord, I pray that You would sow seeds of hope and open my spirit to receive them because I know I need the renewal that comes from You.

But—
When God our Savior revealed his kindness and love, he saved us, not because of the righteous things we had done, but because of his mercy. He washed away our sins, giving us a new birth and new life through the Holy Spirit. He generously poured out the Spirit upon us through Jesus Christ our Savior. Titus 3:4-6 (NLT)

In spite of my confusion, I trust that . . .

APRIL 7

God of this magnificent morning, despite the splendor of creation arrayed all around me, my eyes sometimes fail to see the wonder of a single gardenia blossom or the splash of a wave on my toes. Everything seems brighter when I look for You in the center of my life. Thank you for granting me gratitude's eyes to attend to creation's goodness as I truly live within each moment, praising You for it all.

Let the sea and everything in it shout his praise!
Let the earth and all living things join in.
Let the rivers clap their hands in glee!
Let the hills sing out their songs of joy before the LORD.
Psalm 98:7-9a (NLT)

Jupiter, Florida

APRIL 10

Spirit of the Living God, it is my prayer that I would know the power of your grace and the warmth of your presence, so that I would be changed from the inside out. Thank you for the promise of a fresh start, as seeds of renewed faith take root in my furrowed life. I invite You to clear away the dead growth of the past, break up the tangled roots of routine, and stir in the rich nutrients of vision and challenge. Then bury your Word deep within me; cultivate, water, and tend my heart until new life buds and blossoms and flowers.

The seed that fell on good soil represents those who truly hear and understand God's word and produce a harvest of thirty, sixty, or even a hundred times as much as had been planted!" Matthew 13:23 (NLT)

Trout lily, Vermont

APRIL 9

"Pray, and let God worry." Martin Luther

Compassionate Lord, help me cope with the many concerns on my mind—some for my own needs and some for others' burdens. Look beneath my smile and see the needs that I bring. Help me to be courageous enough to bring my whole being to You. I pray that You would light a new fire in the lukewarm embers of my faith, give new life to my worried, weary heart, and help me embrace new beginnings. O Lord, may your grace be sufficient for each and every day as I trust You to guide my ways, through Jesus Christ.

Bend Your ear to me and listen to my words, O Eternal One;
　　hear the deep cry of my heart.
Listen to my call *for help*,
　　my King, my True God;
　　to You *alone* I pray.
O Eternal One, lead me in *the path of* Your righteousness
　　amidst those who wish me harm;
　　make Your way clear to me.
Psalm 5:1-2, 8 (The Voice)

Remake the part of my heart that . . .

APRIL 10

Spirit of the Living God, it is my prayer that I would know the power of your grace and the warmth of your presence, so that I would be changed from the inside out. Thank you for the promise of a fresh start, as seeds of renewed faith take root in my furrowed life. I invite You to clear away the dead growth of the past, break up the tangled roots of routine, and stir in the rich nutrients of vision and challenge. Then bury your Word deep within me; cultivate, water, and tend my heart until new life buds and blossoms and flowers.

The seed that fell on good soil represents those who truly hear and understand God's word and produce a harvest of thirty, sixty, or even a hundred times as much as had been planted!" Matthew 13:23 (NLT)

Trout lily, Vermont

APRIL 7

God of this magnificent morning, despite the splendor of creation arrayed all around me, my eyes sometimes fail to see the wonder of a single gardenia blossom or the splash of a wave on my toes. Everything seems brighter when I look for You in the center of my life. Thank you for granting me gratitude's eyes to attend to creation's goodness as I truly live within each moment, praising You for it all.

Let the sea and everything in it shout his praise!
   Let the earth and all living things join in.
Let the rivers clap their hands in glee!
   Let the hills sing out their songs of joy before the LORD.
Psalm 98:7-9a (NLT)

Laurie Bohlke   107

APRIL 8

All-merciful God, forgive me for those moments and sometimes even those days when I have found myself becoming critical, rigid, and complaining because I know that I am harboring a negative spirit. Once I begin walking down that road, O Lord, other negative attitudes and behaviors seem to follow. Free me from the prison of my own thinking and feeling so that I can turn to You for the transformation I so desperately need. Expand my capacity to care so that my heart would see and love as You love.

In light of all this, here's what I want you to do. While I'm locked up here, a prisoner for the Master, I want you to get out there and walk—better yet, run!—on the road God called you to travel. I don't want any of you sitting around on your hands. I don't want anyone strolling off, down some path that goes nowhere. And mark that you do this with humility and discipline—not in fits and starts, but steadily, pouring yourselves out for each other in acts of love, alert at noticing differences and quick at mending fences.
You were all called to travel on the same road and in the same direction, so stay together, both outwardly and inwardly. Ephesians 4:1-4 (The Message)

I want to walk down the road of . . .

APRIL 11

O Lord of love, thank you for your Holy Spirit, bringing your presence into my longing life. Help me to seek You with a surrendered heart and to pray that your comfort might so deeply abide within me that any lingering fears might be blown away with the powerful strength of your Spirit. My soul longs to know the peace that comes from trusting You moment by moment.

We don't yet see things clearly. We're squinting in a fog, peering through a mist. But it won't be long before the weather clears and the sun shines bright! We'll see it all then, see it all as clearly as God sees us, knowing him directly just as he knows us!

But for right now, until that completeness, we have three things to do to lead us toward that consummation: Trust steadily in God, hope unswervingly, love extravagantly. And the best of the three is love.

1 Corinthians 13:12-13 (The Message)

How can I seek God more often today?

APRIL 12

O God, my Redeemer, teach me when to stand strong and when to sit silent. Help me to discern what I am powerless to change, but also give me the boldness to risk changing what I can change, in my own situation and in the world. Help me to release my fears by taking one step of faith through the fear, and then keep me from the temptation to snatch back what I have entrusted to You.

God, grant us grace to accept with serenity the things that cannot be changed, courage to change the things that should be changed, and the wisdom to distinguish the one from the other. Reinhold Niebuhr

I can take one step in faith by . . .

APRIL 13

God of mercy, the coming days bring a measure of uncertainty. I ask for courage for the hard times and strength for the challenging tasks that lie before me. But, Lord, I pray not just that I might endure. I ask that even as a grain of sand in the oyster shell becomes by patience and your touch, a pearl, so may my troubles become a means of grace to glorify You. Through the troubles of life, teach me what a faithful God You are. I release my anxieties to You as I place my hand in yours and walk into the future, knowing that it will be good because You are the center of it.

Be strong. Take courage. Don't be intimidated. Don't give them a second thought because GOD, your God, is striding ahead of you. He's right there with you. He won't let you down; he won't leave you.
Deuteronomy 31:6 (The Message)

Mourning dove, Tucson, Arizona

O Lord of all, the Architect of heaven and earth, and the Artisan who crafted each one of your children, your work invites me to whisper, "O Lord, how great Thou art." I offer grateful thanks for prayers answered in a heartbeat or after a long delay, for love renewed, for hope restored, and for faith given wings.

I turn to You to reflect on this week—to celebrate the ways I have scattered seeds of grace but also to acknowledge the ways I have diminished myself and others. For whatever I have brought with me that needs your restoration and healing, I come humbly, open to the truth. I want to be honest before You, willing to allow You to be at work remaking me. Forgive me and set me on a path that calls for the best within me and therefore honors You.

My hands have made both heaven and earth;
*   they and everything in them are mine.*
*   I, the LORD, have spoken!*
* I will bless those who have humble and contrite hearts,*
*   who tremble at my word.*
Isaiah 66:2 (NLT)

Lord, You are great because . . .

APRIL 15

Lord of life, I am swept up by the extravagance of your grace and humbly receive your love. I know that your grace embraces me, especially when I feel unworthy to receive it. Yet, I also confess my doubts. I am awed by your power that created the complexity of the universe, yet I am sometimes surprised by your power that raised Jesus from the dead. Teach me how to trust what I do not yet see because I trust the One who created it all.

(The boy's father said) *"But if you can do anything, take pity on us and help us."*
"If you can?" said Jesus. "Everything is possible for one who believes."
Immediately the boy's father exclaimed, "I do believe; help me overcome my unbelief!" Mark 9:22b-24 (NIV)

In what areas of my life do I want to grow in trust?

APRIL 16

God of great compassion, my heart aches with the news flashes and all-too-vivid portraits of pain in the world. I have such difficulty comprehending how some could have such callous disregard for human suffering. Convert my anger and pain into a thirst for God-like justice. Precious Lord, embrace those who have been devastated by loss and pain and hold them close in your everlasting arms. Help them to know with the depth of their being that they are known and loved and cherished in your eyes and that your strength is their sustenance.

Go ahead and be angry. You do well to be angry—but don't use your anger as fuel for revenge. And don't stay angry. Don't go to bed angry. Don't give the Devil that kind of foothold in your life. Ephesians 4:26 (The Message)

Ring-necked duck, Tampa, Florida   Jeff Wendorff

APRIL 17

There are times in all of our lives when it is particularly difficult to pray, and I find that in those times it is always a Scripture verse that I focus on. Perhaps, the one that I love the most is, "Be still and know that I am God." No more than that. It reminds me that God is with me.

I also use it as a short meditation, dropping words each time I say the verse.

Be still and know that I am God.

Be still and know that I am.

Be still and know.

Be still.

Be.

Ever-present God, sometimes I don't know what I need, but You somehow reach out to me in a multitude of ways—touching me, healing me, encouraging me through your love.

Be still, and know that I am God!
  I will be honored by every nation.
  I will be honored throughout the world.
Psalm 46:10 (NLT)

I know God is with me when . . .

APRIL 18

Blessed Lord, when I pause to seek You, your presence is like a fountain in a thirsty land, or bright sunshine after a storm, or the arms of a friend at an anticipated homecoming, and gratitude wraps around me. I thank You for the wisdom of maturity that helps me to look back with eyes of grace and acceptance, remembering the truly important parts of life. This day, I celebrate life ready to be explored, joy waiting to be unwrapped, and beauty hiding in plain sight.

Knowing what is right is like deep water in the heart;
a wise person draws from the well within.
Proverbs 20:5 (The Message)

When do I detect unrecognized beauty?

APRIL 19

O God of the wounded heart, on distant shores are people for whom each day is a struggle. All the troubles swirling around in our world cry out for healing. There are the places where violence and war prevail, where human suffering seems without end, where situations of fear or injustice or hatred seem to defy human solutions. I pray that You would be at work bringing hope for hurt, clarity for confusion, and solutions out of impossibilities. In times when it is difficult to be hopeful, remind me that You always provide a path where there seems to be none. O Lord, make me an instrument of peace, a messenger of hope, and a whisperer of prayer.

For nothing will be impossible with God. Luke 1:37 (ESV)

Uganda

APRIL 20

Shepherd of my soul, guide me through the coming week as I journey together with You. As I pray, I seek to quiet myself and become so aware of your presence that I can keep my focus on You, never losing my way. I want to tune in to the power and wisdom of your Holy Spirit, allowing You to blow through my defenses and change the parts of my life that have created barriers in my relationship with You and with the ones I love. I pray that I might be open to your gift of the Holy Spirit, offering me the strength I need to journey even deeper into the way of Jesus, my Lord.

With your unfailing love you lead
*   the people you have redeemed.*
In your might, you guide them
*   to your sacred home.*
Exodus 15:13 (NLT)

I need strength to . . .

APRIL 21

A special friend reminded me this week of how important it is to make time for quiet moments because the world is very loud—and God usually speaks to us in whispers.

Lord of all life, clear away the cobwebs of my tangled thoughts and the confusion of all the competing noises, so that I might leave them for just this moment to truly connect with You. In the quietness of this moment, I want to be sensitive enough to
hear the whispers of your affirmation,
see the puzzle pieces of my life shifting into place,
and experience life priorities realigning to honor You.

The LORD is in his holy temple; let all the earth be silent before him.
Habakkuk 2:20 (NIV)

In this quiet moment I can . . .

APRIL 22

Eternal God, thank you for all the goodness with which You fill my life: rising suns and evening dusk, blue crystal skies and roaring surf, children growing, and the compassion and wisdom of my elders. I worship You, for I know that You are the center of my existence. You meet me in prayer as I seek to honor You in the name of the one who leads me to You, my Lord Jesus Christ.

I lift you high in praise, my God, O my King!
*   and I'll bless your name into eternity.*
I'll bless you every day,
*   and keep it up from now to eternity.*
God is magnificent; he can never be praised enough.
There are no boundaries to his greatness.
Psalm 145:1-3 (The Message)

Santorini, Greece

APRIL 23

God of grace, at times I hesitate to admit the depth of my need for You. I may be reluctant to acknowledge the limits of my self-sufficiency and may struggle to realize that true freedom comes from letting go and trusting in your goodness and your will. I confess the ways I have turned away from You in my busyness, my self-absorption, and my blindness to others' needs. I turn to You now asking your forgiveness. I know I need healing for my soul and peace for my spirit. Come to me now to receive my confession and to grant healing so that I might be made whole again.

He is so rich in kindness and grace that he purchased our freedom with the blood of his Son and forgave our sins. Ephesians 1:7 (NLT)

Forgive me for . . .

APRIL 24

Ever-renewing God, as I rest in your holiness, I come with an open heart, anticipating that You will have a word for me today, that I might hear what I need to hear through Scripture or song or prayer or the words of someone I meet. Whenever I am in your presence, I admit a hope stirs within me that You will reach out and meet my needs in ways I cannot even articulate. I simply want to experience that You are closer than I can imagine.

Send out your light and your truth;
*   let them guide me.*
Let them lead me to your holy mountain,
*   to the place where you live.*
There I will go to the altar of God,
*   to God—the source of all my joy.*
I will praise you with my harp,
*   O God, my God!*
Psalm 43:3-4 (NLT)

As I open my heart and mind to God's word today, I hear . . .

APRIL 25

Everlasting Lord, your glory is proclaimed in the beautiful abundance of your created order. Wherever I look, your artistry beckons me to praise. Today, enable me to see your inventiveness in the unexpected brilliance of wildflowers by an ancient tree stump, or in the red patch on the blackbird's wing, or in the dance of light on the surface of the water. Save me from the ease of indifference, and grant me the vision to discover your presence and revel in your goodness.

Give thanks to the LORD, for he is good,
  for his steadfast love endures forever.
Psalm 136:1 (ESV)

Indian paintbrush, Utah

APRIL 26

Holy Spirit, I enter this time of prayer with a sense of anticipation and hope that your presence will nourish and encourage and strengthen me today. O Lord, I am hungry and thirsty for your Word of life. You call out to me with the gift of solitude so that I might step back from the turbulence of the times to reflect on the direction of my life. I am grateful for the sacred moments when my soul has been restored by your peace.

"Don't be afraid," he said, *"for you are very precious to God. Peace! Be encouraged! Be strong!"*
As he spoke these words to me, I suddenly felt stronger and said to him, "Please speak to me, my lord, for you have strengthened me."
Daniel 10:19 (NLT)

I need God's strength in . . .

APRIL 27

It's so important to know in our hearts that grace is the very opposite of merit. To know that we are unconditionally loved regardless of our accomplishments is an unearned gift from God.

O God, I come before You with a wide open heart, ready to surrender the stones of guilt and judgment and self-criticism to receive your gifts of compassion and love. When I am honest, I admit that it is hard for me to imagine the depth and breadth of your mercy. You embrace me in the moments when I feel the most unworthy of your acceptance. Yet, it is in those times most of all that You wrap me in the arms of your grace and remind me of my value to You. I ask that You would empower me with your mercy as I trust in the power of my Lord, Jesus Christ, who died to make everything new in my life.

But you, O LORD,
*   are a God of compassion and mercy,*
slow to get angry
*   and filled with unfailing love and faithfulness.*
Psalm 86:15 (NLT)

When do I need God's comfort?

APRIL 28

Lord of all creation, I pause with gratitude for both the spectacular and the simple gifts around me as I anticipate a new day with a deep breath and a fresh hope. You have splashed your blessings in my life—a brisk walk in the coolness before dawn's first light, the blissful embrace of sunshine's warmth as I enjoy a forest trail, the simple contentment of feeling at home in your creation, and the peace that abides as I rest in your grace.

But I will sing of your strength;
  I will sing aloud of your steadfast love in the morning.
For you have been to me a fortress
  and a refuge in the day of my distress.
Psalm 59:16 (ESV)

Danby, Vermont

APRIL 29

Precious Redeemer, I know that I often live as if Easter never happened, filled with regrets about the past, or immersed in worries instead of hope about the future. Teach me to live completely in this moment, trusting You to make all things new in my life, teaching me how to live more courageously, more expectantly, more joyfully. Empower me to live with the passion of the first believers who witnessed the resurrection and began to live life with abandon and power, trusting that with You, Lord, nothing is impossible.

So be strong and courageous,
all you who put your hope in the LORD!
Psalm 31:24 (NLT)

I could live my life more courageously by . . .

APRIL 30

O Comforting God, open the eyes of my heart to see people through the eyes of Jesus. I am reminded of his tears of compassion for his people. Lord, I know that there are

> those who feel weak,
> those who know the ache of loneliness,
> those who are grieving,
> those who are imprisoned,
> and those who are deeply confused about the direction of their lives.

My heart is with the many whose fears weigh on their minds. Reach out with the tender touch of your Spirit to grant your peace. Help me to walk with You, giving me a vision of the redeeming power of sacrificial love and of the eternal triumph of life over death.

I am leaving you with a gift—peace of mind and heart. And the peace I give is a gift the world cannot give. So don't be troubled or afraid. John 14:27 (NLT)

How can I offer to peace to others today?

MAY 1

O God of this day and all moments in time, my heart is hushed as I pause to give You thanks. When unexpected laughter bubbles up, I see your hand at work. I am grateful. When an unexpected kindness brushes against my isolation, your grace takes me by surprise. I am grateful. You meet me in the most ordinary moments of life, and I find myself humbled by a love that is unlike anything I have ever known. I am grateful. You look deep within and remind me that I am precious and wonderful in your sight. Above all, I am grateful.

How precious is your unfailing love, O God!
All humanity finds shelter
*   in the shadow of your wings.*
Psalm 36:7 (NLT)

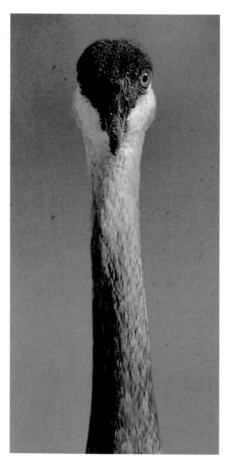

Sandhill Crane, New Mexico Jeff Wendorff

MAY 2

O Bread of Life, I come before You, humbly ready to receive your Word. As I reflect on celebrating the Lord's supper, I am touched once again by how You take the crumbs of my life and work miracles in and through me as I surrender all into your care. At the table, remind me once again that You will sustain me day by day as I trust You for bread enough to replenish my soul for one day's journey with You.

As they were eating, Jesus took some bread and blessed it. Then he broke it in pieces and gave it to the disciples, saying, "Take this and eat it, for this is my body."
And he took a cup of wine and gave thanks to God for it. He gave it to them and said, "Each of you drink from it, for this is my blood, which confirms the covenant between God and his people. It is poured out as a sacrifice to forgive the sins of many. Matthew 26:26-28 (NLT)

Lord, I surrender . . .

MAY 3

When Jesus' disciples asked Jesus how to pray, this is how The Message interprets what he said to them: *"Here's what I want you to do. Find a quiet, secluded place so you won't be tempted to role play before God. Just be there as simply and honestly as you can manage. The focus will shift from you to God, and you will begin to sense his grace."* Matthew 6:6 The Message

Lord of the quiet whisper, teach me the joy of stillness so that I might come to You now as I really am—with no masks and no pretensions. Embrace me and encourage me, granting me enough trust to listen and enough strength to surrender my will to yours.

Be still, my soul: begin the song of praise
On earth, believing, to Thy Lord on high;
Acknowledge Him in all thy words and ways,
So shall He view thee with a well pleased eye.
Be still, my soul: the Sun of life divine
Through passing clouds shall but more brightly shine.
Catharina von Schlegal, 1752

My favorite place to pray is . . .

MAY 4

Thank you, O Lord of all creation, as I watch the morning sun suddenly emerge across the distant horizon awakening me to a new day filled with promise. I know the power of the promise that your mercies are fresh every morning. Great is your faithfulness. I pray with faith and hope because You have already blessed my life so richly. You have again provided exactly what I have needed. Your love for me is real and reaches to the ends of the earth. As your Word proclaims, I can go nowhere that You are not already waiting for me, ready to meet me and to lead me back home.

The steadfast love of the LORD never ceases;
his mercies never come to an end;
they are new every morning;
great is your faithfulness.
Lamentations 3:22-23 (ESV)

Stonington Harbor, Maine

MAY 5

All-knowing God, we come from many different places, yet each one yearns to know your presence. Underneath it all, I long for so much more—more meaning for each day, a sense of purpose for my life, a peace that will surround me constantly. You have touched me with a tap on the shoulder, beckoned with the right word at the right time, and opened a door to allow the discovery of a life beyond anything ever imagined.

Even today, You haven't stopped reaching out. You surprise me in my tracks with an unexpected opportunity. You answer prayers that I haven't begun to imagine praying. You are always one step ahead of me, devising plans that will bring me life and hope and a future. You are, indeed, an awesome God.

As Jesus walked beside the Sea of Galilee, he saw Simon and his brother Andrew casting a net into the lake, for they were fishermen. "Come, follow me," Jesus said, "and I will send you out to fish for people." At once they left their nets and followed him. Mark 1:16-18 (NIV)

Your encouragement leads me to . . .

MAY 6

Lord of comfort, remind me that even when I cannot see your hand at work, I can still trust your heart. And so, I turn to You because You are my fortress and my present strength in times of trouble. It is my heartfelt prayer that You would reach out to each one who feels bruised by the buffeting of grief or battered by the wounds that life can bring. I pray for the ones who have been hurt by thoughtlessness or wearied by strife. Encourage each one, granting rest and strength to get through each day. As I begin my day, in your presence, help me to know your peace as I place these burdens in your hands.

Those who live in the shelter of the Most High
*   will find rest in the shadow of the Almighty.*
This I declare about the LORD:
He alone is my refuge, my place of safety;
*   he is my God, and I trust him.*
Psalm 91:1-2 (NLT)

I want healing peace for . . .

MAY 7

Calming Spirit, a thousand thoughts are tumbling through my mind. It is so easy to simply drift in my life, away from You and your priorities for me. Starting today, help me put away my cares and anxieties, my concern for image and pleasing others, and my preoccupation with the unnecessary and fleeting so that I can fix my mind only on You. Then allow your Word to break through to restore and empower me to live the life You envision for me.

And why do you worry about clothes? See how the flowers of the field grow. They do not labor or spin. Yet I tell you that not even Solomon in all his splendor was dressed like one of these. If that is how God clothes the grass of the field, which is here today and tomorrow is thrown into the fire, will he not much more clothe you—you of little faith? So do not worry, saying, 'What shall we eat?' or 'What shall we drink?' or 'What shall we wear?'
Matthew 6:28-31 (NIV)

Texas hill country

MAY 8

Great Comforter, on this Mother's Day, I lift up all mothers and pray that You may richly bless them with your strength, patience, love, and wisdom because I know that sometimes life is hard. Thank you, Lord, for my family, the ones with whom I share a home and those who have provided a heritage for me. I am grateful for the special people in my life who have not only challenged me to discover my uniqueness but have also encouraged me to reach beyond myself to offer the world my gifts. They have provided a living example of their faith for me and have reminded me that I am loved by You.

(The Apostle Paul wrote) I am reminded of your sincere faith, a faith that lived first in your grandmother Lois and your mother Eunice and now, I am sure, lives in you. For this reason I remind you to rekindle the gift of God that is within you through the laying on of my hands; for God did not give us a spirit of cowardice, but rather a spirit of power and of love and of self-discipline.
2 Timothy 1:5-7 (NSRV)

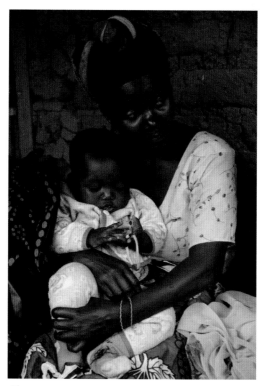

Tanzania   Brenda Berry

MAY 9

Lord of all, who crafted massive redwood trees and delicate lilac blossoms, towering giraffes and tiny tadpoles, help me to stop long enough to glory in what my eyes observe and my ears perceive—to live in the sheer excitement of being alive. Surprise me today, O Lord, with your unsurpassing goodness. Help my heart sense and seek the joy of a life abiding in You; help my spirit drink in the beauty of a world You made for my delight.

For the Beauty of the Earth

For the beauty of the earth,
For the beauty of the skies,
For the love which from our birth
Over and around us lies,
Lord of all, to thee we raise
This our grateful hymn of praise.

For the beauty of each hour
Of the day and of the night,
Hill and vale, and tree and flower,
Sun and moon and stars of light,
Lord of all, to thee we raise
This our grateful hymn of praise.
Folliott S. Pierpoint 1864

I am surprised by . . .

MAY 10

O God of infinite patience, I come before You with an honest and pure spirit. I try to seek what is right, but sometimes it is more comfortable to do what is easy. I try my best to avoid hurting the ones I love, but sometimes I find myself impatient and critical. So often I do exactly what I vowed not to do and avoid the good I intend to do. Work deep within me, encouraging me by giving me the strength to do your will.

I can anticipate the response that is coming: "I know that all God's commands are spiritual, but I'm not. Isn't this also your experience?" Yes. I'm full of myself—after all, I've spent a long time in sin's prison. What I don't understand about myself is that I decide one way, but then I act another, doing things I absolutely despise. So if I can't be trusted to figure out what is best for myself and then do it, it becomes obvious that God's command is necessary. Romans 7:14-16 (The Message)

Work deep within me, Lord, to . . .

MAY 11

Life-changing Lord, teach me to wait with You in quiet ways as I invite You to refashion my character so that I might serve others freely. As I pray today, teach me to see with new eyes the wonders that lie right at my doorstep. Take away my weariness, my habit of not being present, my dullness to what is beautiful and holy. Increase my sensitivity to the people around me so that You might use my gifts to be a blessing to them, in the name of your Son, Jesus Christ.

In his grace, God has given us different gifts for doing certain things well. So if God has given you the ability to prophesy, speak out with as much faith as God has given you. If your gift is serving others, serve them well. If you are a teacher, teach well. If your gift is to encourage others, be encouraging. If it is giving, give generously. If God has given you leadership ability, take the responsibility seriously. And if you have a gift for showing kindness to others, do it gladly. Romans 12:6-8 (NLT)

What are my unique gifts?

I often choose to read the Bible through an ancient process called *Lexio Divina* (sacred reading). In this experience, I read the Bible passage four different times to hear what the Spirit is saying to me in the present moment.

#1 Simply read it aloud slowly and hear the words clearly for your own life.
#2 Read it again. Focus on the word or phrase that captures your attention.
#3 Read it again. Ask God how this phrase speaks to your life at this moment.
#4 Read it once more and just listen for God's response.

God of abundant life, as I reflect on Scripture this week, may the words You have inspired be touched with vibrancy, renewing my life by the power of your Holy Spirit. May the wisdom of the Word bring new meaning to my everyday life. As I read, Lord, enable me to hear a word of encouragement or a new challenge, and to take a step to follow You more closely.

As it is written in the Scriptures, "They will all be taught by God." Everyone who listens to the Father and learns from him comes to me. John 6:45 (NLT)

One of the Bible verses that has great meaning for me is . . .

MAY 13

God of glory, thank you for all of creation's treasures—for the freshness of the wind, for the fragrance of spring, and for the sun that brings all the shapes and splashes of color to light. I remember the gifts of this week—a small kindness, a gentle touch, an understanding smile, a child's belly laugh. I thank you for the deep sense of peace that arises within me as I make time to be with You in prayer.

As the deer pants for streams of water,
*   so my souls pants for you, my God.*
My soul thirsts for God, for the living God.
*   When can I go and meet with God?*
Psalm 42:1-2 (NIV)

Londonderry, Vermont

MAY 14

Almighty God, Maker of heaven and earth, thank you for reminding me that I count with You. I stand amazed that amid all the galaxies of the universe, your heart holds mine in love. Whenever I stumble or fall, I know that You are always there with your outstretched hand holding mine, encouraging me to walk in step with You. Help me to know from the depths of my being that circumstances in my life do not have to control me if I can trust You to lead me through them.

Bless the Eternal!
   For He has revealed His gracious love to me
   when I was trapped like a city under siege.
I began to panic so I yelled out,
   "I'm cut off. You no longer see me!"
But You heard my cry for help *that day*
   when I called out to You.
Psalm 31:21-22 (The Voice)

I trust God now to . . .

MAY 15

Prince of Peace, through this time of prayer, I seek to quiet myself so that I might be sensitive to the still, small voice of your Holy Spirit—allowing it to blow through my defenses and truly transform me. Living by your Spirit gives me the strength I need to journey even deeper into the way of Jesus, my Lord. Your Spirit empowers me to seek to change the parts of my life that have become obstructions in my relationship with You and with the ones I love. At times I feel unable to make the changes needed, and yet You grant me the grace to take small steps of faith. Each small step deepens my trust that your power is at work within me doing more than I could ask or imagine.

So now there is no condemnation for those who belong to Christ Jesus. And because you belong to him, the power of the life-giving Spirit has freed you from the power of sin that leads to death. Romans 8:1-2 NLT

The part of my life I want to change is . . .

MAY 16

Lord God, help me to trust You when the road becomes rocky, and especially when it descends suddenly into the deep, shadowy valleys of despair, depression, or death. I ask that your presence be with each one who knows the depths of this valley today. And when the view from the mountaintops of life is so beautiful that it takes my breath away, I want to recognize that You are the source of all creation, the beginning and end of my journey, the God of grace, compassion, and love. And I praise You for it all.

Even in the *unending* shadows of death's darkness,
   I am not overcome by fear.
Because You are with me *in those dark moments*,
   near with Your protection and guidance,
   I am comforted.
Psalm 23:4 (The Voice)

Denali National Park, Alaska

MAY 17

Thank you for being a God who invites me to come to You fearlessly. I am so grateful that You meet my mustard-seed faith with your steadfast love and mercy, moving in ways that are beyond my wildest dreams. I ask You to forgive my doubting when I am afraid to trust your goodness. Draw me into your presence this day as I take steps of faith into the embrace of your love.

Then Jesus rebuked the demon in the boy, and it left him. From that moment the boy was well.
Afterward the disciples asked Jesus privately, "Why couldn't we cast out that demon?"
"You don't have enough faith," Jesus told them. "I tell you the truth, if you had faith even as small as a mustard seed, you could say to this mountain, 'Move from here to there,' and it would move. Nothing would be impossible."
Matthew 17:18-20 (NLT)

For me a step of faith would be . . .

The great Quaker leader, George Fox said: "Walk joyfully on the earth and respond to that of God in every human being." That is especially good advice when I am dealing with the difficult people in my life.

Wonderful Counselor, I ask that You would help me with the relationships in my life that are sometimes challenging. When I find myself bombarded by criticism or unreasonable expectations, when I find myself ignored or bent to another's will, remind me of your grace and lead me to see others in the light of your love. Teach me when to speak with conviction and when to let go in gracious acceptance. Remind me that at times You use even those who are difficult to teach me about myself. Teach me to be still, Lord, that I may truly hear my brothers and sisters, and through them, your voice.

"You're familiar with the old written law, 'Love your friend,' and its unwritten companion, 'Hate your enemy.' I'm challenging that. I'm telling you to love your enemies. Let them bring out the best in you, not the worst. When someone gives you a hard time, respond with the energies of prayer, for then you are working out of your true selves, your God-created selves. This is what God does. He gives his best—the sun to warm and the rain to nourish—to everyone, regardless: the good and bad, the nice and nasty. If all you do is love the lovable, do you expect a bonus? Anybody can do that. If you simply say hello to those who greet you, do you expect a medal? Any run-of-the-mill sinner does that."
"In a word, what I'm saying is, Grow up. You're kingdom subjects. Now live like it. Live out your God-created identity. Live generously and graciously toward others, the way God lives toward you." Matthew 5:43-48 (The Message)

I want to listen more to . . .

MAY 19

O Lord of refreshment, I am thirsty for that living water that You have promised me through your Holy Spirit. I yearn to grasp deeper truths, to listen beyond familiar words to find new meaning for today. I dare to seek, and in so doing, to find a ray of light in the darkness or an insight far beyond my own wisdom. If I am honest with myself, I admit I don't really want earth-shaking, lightning-bolt change. I just want to be closer to You, step-by-step, changing my heart beat-by-beat.

My child, pay attention to what I say.
* Listen carefully to my words.*
Don't lose sight of them.
* Let them penetrate deep into your heart,*
for they bring life to those who find them,
* and healing to their whole body.*
  Proverbs 4:20-22 (NLT)

Glen Lake, Vermont

MAY 20

I remember, O Lord, that your Church was born because of your Holy Spirit alive among an expectant people. Thank you for touching the Body of Christ with a dose of your infectious enthusiasm. Your Spirit is alive and at work. Help me to keep my heart open as I seek to know your will and do your work in your Church and in my community.

On the day of Pentecost all the believers were meeting together in one place. Suddenly, there was a sound from heaven like the roaring of a mighty windstorm, and it filled the house where they were sitting. Then, what looked like flames or tongues of fire appeared and settled on each of them. And everyone present was filled with the Holy Spirit and began speaking in other languages, as the Holy Spirit gave them this ability.

At that time there were devout Jews from every nation living in Jerusalem. When they heard the loud noise, everyone came running, and they were bewildered to hear their own languages being spoken by the believers.

They were completely amazed. "How can this be?" they exclaimed. "These people are all from Galilee, and yet we hear them speaking in our own native languages! . . .

And we all hear these people speaking in our own language about the wonderful things God has done!" Acts 2:1-8, 11 (NLT)

Where do I need the Holy Spirit's presence in my life?

MAY 21

Gracious God, today I pray for humility. Comfort me as I move toward setting my agenda aside so that your will might take center stage in my life. Teach me today how to let go of

my resentments over past wrongs,

my guilt over poor choices,

my envy over what others may have,

and my expectations of others.

I also ask You to teach me how to hang on—to a faith that can move a mountain, to a hope in your goodness triumphing in the end, and to a trust that when I seek your will, I will find it. Help me to pray with passion the prayer You always answer: Lord, make me more like You.

You who are younger *in the faith*: do as your elders *and leaders* ask. All of you should treat each other with humility, *for as it says in Proverbs,*

God opposes the proud

But offers grace to the humble. 1 Peter 5:5 (The Voice)

Where does my pride prevent me from letting go?

MAY 22

O Lord, my God, my prayers encircle those who need your healing embrace—for those I love who are navigating long journeys of illness and grueling treatments, for the ones who carry burdens of doubt or disappointment, for each one who seeks You in the midst of challenging circumstances. For I know You are the Shepherd who rescues each of us from days of darkness to bring us to the pastures of springtime.

The one who enters by the gate is the shepherd of the sheep. The gatekeeper opens the gate for him, and the sheep listen to his voice. He calls his own sheep by name and leads them out. When he has brought out all his own, he goes on ahead of them, and his sheep follow him because they know his voice. John 10:2-4 (NIV)

Israel   Tisa Queen-Oldham

MAY 23

Blessed Lord, thank you for those who have cared enough to speak the truth in love to me. Thank you for the insight that comes after struggles, for wisdom and maturity that sometimes come the hard way, and for all the grace-filled second chances I have been given. Thank you for those who walk with me showing me that You don't just call extraordinary people to follow Jesus—You call ordinary people and You make them extraordinary.

A person standing alone can be attacked and defeated, but two can stand back-to-back and conquer. Three are even better, for a triple-braided cord is not easily broken. Ecclesiastes 4:12 (NLT)

I am blessed with friends who . . .

MAY 24

God of infinite patience, I want quick answers, but You seem to work slowly and deliberately. I live marginless and harried, but You seem to urge me to live in the present, trusting You to provide all that I need as I surrender to You. Help me to live with the power of your Spirit so that I might have the courage to face any obstacles and finally trust You to bring a victory over the most impossible circumstances. In the name of Jesus, I pray.

Bend down, O LORD, and hear my prayer;
  answer me, for I need your help.
Protect me, for I am devoted to you.
  Save me, for I serve you and trust you.
  You are my God.
Be merciful to me, O Lord,
  for I am calling on you constantly.
Psalm 86:1-3 (NLT)

I need the courage to . . .

MAY 25

Abba God, who watches over me with endless love and care, thank you for the wonders that lie before me on this journey of life. With the promise of your loving presence deep in my soul, I lift to You the joys in my life: the renewal of old friendships, children and youth discovering simple outdoor joys, a word of encouragement offered when I need it most. Teach me the art of seeing much, hearing much, and loving much. Give me the ability to wake up each morning grateful to be fully aware and alive. Day by day I proclaim your faithfulness in quiet praise.

Your unfailing love is better than life itself;
how I praise you!
I will praise you as long as I live,
lifting up my hands to you in prayer.
You satisfy me more than the richest feast.
I will praise you with songs of joy.
Psalm 63:3-5 (NLT)

Bainbridge Island, Washington   Brenda Berry

MAY 26

O Lord of abundant life, You have protected our youth beneath the shadow of your wings. You have tenderly led them and encouraged them to take the next step of faith as they transition from one chapter of life to another. As they contemplate their futures, grant them the gift of enthusiasm for the journey ahead. Surround them with your constant presence. I pray that each one might hear You call them by name, reminding them that they are yours today and each day of their lives. I pray that You will pour out your Spirit upon them, helping them to grow in deepening wisdom and in daring courage that You might use their willing hearts to make a difference for You in their worlds.

I will instruct you and teach you in the way you should go;
 I will counsel you with my loving eye on you.
Psalm 32:8 (NIV)

I pray for . . .

MAY 27

God of grace, You have given me special people to love, so lead me to offer my love in concrete acts of service today. If I am harboring resentments, give me the willingness to forgive another. If I am limping along without a spark of passion, plant a hope for new-found joy deep within me. O Healing One, make whole the ragged parts of my life and grant the balm of your peace.

Summing up: Be agreeable, be sympathetic, be loving, be compassionate, be humble. That goes for all of you, no exceptions. No retaliation. No sharp-tongued sarcasm. Instead, bless—that's your job, to bless. You'll be a blessing and also get a blessing. 1 Peter 3:8 (The Message)

What passions has God placed within me?

MAY 28

Dear Lord, on this weekend I remember the gift of the sacrifice of so many for the freedom this nation cherishes. Help me to be mindful that freedom sometimes comes at tremendous cost so that I never take that gift for granted. I am grateful for each person who gave of themselves and am truly thankful for the blessings that freedom offers. Help me to live with intention and purpose, prayerful always that justice will prevail, not just in my nation, but in every corner of this world.

It is absolutely clear that God has called you to a free life. Just make sure that you don't use this freedom as an excuse to do whatever you want to do and destroy your freedom. Rather, use your freedom to serve one another in love; that's how freedom grows. For everything we know about God's Word is summed up in a single sentence: Love others as you love yourself. That's an act of true freedom. Galatians 5:13-14 (The Message)

MAY 29

I have come to this time of prayer, Lord, not out of any sense of obligation but because of my deep need for your mercy and grace. Remove the blinders of denial from my eyes so that I might see myself as You see me—imperfect and flawed, but also crafted for your purposes. As I surrender my doubts, resentments, hurts, fears, and anger into your hands, You take the broken pieces of my life and create something authentic and beautiful that will touch this world with a measure of your grace.

I think of God, and I moan,
  overwhelmed with longing for his help.
Psalm 77:3 (NLT)

I can no longer deny that . . .

MAY 30

Usually my prayers are full of words telling God everything that God already knows is in my heart, but spending precious little time listening for what God wants me to hear.

Gentle God, I come to meet You in a quiet place to re-center my spirit in a noisy world. I want to spend time in prayer so that I can talk with You, and in meditation so that I can listen for your answers. Help me to experience the sacredness of each moment You give me as I kneel before You with an open heart.

Pay attention, Job, and listen to me;
  be silent, and I will speak.
Job 33:31 (NIV)

How can I create patches of silence in my day?

MAY 31

Eternal and loving Lord, through the warmth of the spring sunshine and the blessing of the afternoon rain, all creation awakens and blossoms into a bounty of color. You who breathed this world into being also crafted the precision of a hummingbird's wing, the glory of a mountain range, and the warmth of a child's hand in my own. Your grace is near, O Lord, for You are the God of all life. You wait in silence for me until I open my heart to You in prayer.

God arms me with strength,
    and he makes my way perfect.
He makes me as surefooted as a deer,
    enabling me to stand on mountain heights.
Psalm 18:32-33 (NLT)

Olympic National Park, Washington

Lord of the sea and the land, I have seen your majesty in the rising morning mists, in the afternoon's glow against the ocean blue, and in the shadows of evening spreading across the land. I pray that You might gift me with a fresh outpouring of your Spirit today, for I know You are with me on the peaks of my joys, on the pathways of my daily life, and at the crossroads of my choices.

The human spirit is the lamp of the LORD that sheds light on one's inmost being.
Proverbs 20:27 (NIV)

Versailles, Kentucky

I love to write in my journal. One day as I was writing, I noticed I was using words like *afraid, anxious,* and *inadequate.* I realized that those feelings are my signal that an opportunity to learn something from God awaits me. For me, it is almost always trust. Trusting in God removes my worries.

Dear God, take my hand and teach me the secret of living just one day at a time. I believe that each new day brings with it the possibility of so much joy that I cannot fully explore it, so many blessings that I cannot even count them, and just enough hope that I know I can trust You.

We put our hope in the LORD.
  He is our help and our shield.
In him our hearts rejoice,
  for we trust in his holy name.
Let your unfailing love surround us, LORD,
  for our hope is in you alone.
Psalm 33:20-22 (NLT)

I trust God to transform me by . . .

JUNE 3

O God of tenderness, I lift up all the thoughts stirring within me. I pray for my relationships—those that are enriching as well as those that are troubling. Where I need to release hurts or resentments, I ask that You would give me the desire and the ability to let them go. Where I need to reach out in affirmation to ones around me, give me just the right words of encouragement. Lead me to respond to your call to be a change-maker in my own sphere of influence as I share my gifts with those I know. I ask all this in the name of the One who is my strength and my peace, Jesus Christ my Lord.

And when you stand praying, if you hold anything against anyone, forgive them, so that your Father in heaven may forgive you your sins. Mark 11:25 (NIV)

Where can I use my gifts today?

JUNE 4

O Lord of all creation, You bless me with the beauty of my five senses, and today I celebrate the gift of sound. I thank You for the enveloping echoes of nature—for the music of a tumbling waterfall, for the rustle of the fresh breezes of summertime, and for the harmony of voices and instruments that celebrate your majesty in song. Thank you for your constant reminder that your blessings are all around me when I can shift my attention from petty problems and begin to give thanks for all that is good in my life.

Let the whole world bless our God
and loudly sing his praises.
Psalm 66:8 (NLT)

Olympic National Park, Washington

Precious Lord, You remind me often that life is more than worrying about my own life—it is reaching out to others with the grace that You have given to me. So I offer my own life to You now in service. In those moments You place before me, in the opportunities You give me for hidden serving, empower me to offer a random act of kindness with no need for human affirmation, living for an audience of One—for You, Lord.

But among you it will be different. Whoever wants to be a leader among you must be your servant, and whoever wants to be first among you must become your slave. For even the Son of Man came not to be served but to serve others and to give his life as a ransom for many. Matthew 20: 26-28 (NLT)

Today a random act of kindness might be . . .

O Spirit of calm courage, I lift to You in prayer those who find themselves in lonely valleys where the shadows linger and those who are engulfed in a darkness that seems to be impenetrable to even a glimmer of light. I pray for those bound by life circumstances that are breaking their spirits. In every situation that is beyond my control, I turn to You, praying that by the touch of your hand, each one might be set free. It is my deepest prayer that your peace would enfold this world, touching it with a glimpse of your Kingdom always.

Have mercy on me, O God, have mercy!
   I look to you for protection.
I will hide beneath the shadow of your wings
   until the danger passes by.
Psalm 57:1 (NLT)

Which concerns in my life do I need to release to God in prayer?

JUNE 7

Lord of the universe, I am grateful for those moments when I experience the inconceivable surprise of living—those eternal instants of grace-filled awe that always lead me back to You. I celebrate the wind rippling through a grassy meadow, a baby animal basking in the sunshine, and children spinning in dizzied joy. And then I pause for just one moment, breathe in, and settle into a soft-whispered hallelujah.

Let everything that has breath praise the LORD.
  Praise the LORD.
Psalm 150:6 (NIV)

Baby porcupine, Montana

JUNE 8

With my eyes closed but heart open before You, O Lord, I come to You in the only way I know—through prayer. As my breathing relaxes and my shoulders release their tension, I enter your loving presence more deeply. In this time of connection with your Holy Spirit, I can feel safe and open. And I can dare to reveal my deepest concerns to You, offering them to your healing touch. And in this still, silent moment, I pray for myself, for those most dear to me, and for the world in which I live.

Let the words of my mouth and the meditation of my heart
Be acceptable in your sight,
O Lord, my strength and my Redeemer.
Psalm 19:14 New King James Version (NKJV)

In the quiet I am open to . . .

JUNE 9

God of new beginnings, I am so thankful for the purpose and possibilities You offer to me. Yet, I confess that I have often chosen to follow a path of least resistance rather than turn to You in faith. I have been envious of what I do not have instead of rejoicing in your abundant gifts. I have worried incessantly instead of surrendering those concerns to You in trust. Tender Shepherd, I ask for forgiveness so that I might start anew, trusting in your grace to guide me and lead my heart back home to You this day.

If you, LORD, kept a record of sins,
  LORD, who could stand?
But with you there is forgiveness,
  so that we can, with reverence, serve you.
Psalm 130:3-4 (NIV)

Where do I want to begin anew?

O Lord of life, I am reminded that some moments are so incredibly perfect that they literally take my breath away. So thank you for the beaming smile of a toddler learning the joy of words, for the simple pleasure of gathering at a table with ones I love, and for moments when time seems to stand still and your amazing grace breaks through in my own life.

So I recommend having fun, because there is nothing better for people in this world than to eat, drink, and enjoy life. That way they will experience some happiness along with all the hard work God gives them under the sun.
Ecclesiastes 8:15 (NLT)

Syracuse, New York   Laurie Bohlke   171

Theologian Howard Thurman penned: "Don't ask what the world needs. Ask what makes you come alive and go do it. Because what the world needs is people who have come alive."

Blessed Savior, teach me to live completely in this moment, trusting You to make everything new in my life. Teach me how to live more courageously, more expectantly, and more joyfully. Empower me to live with the passion of the first believers who witnessed the resurrection, who then began to live life with purpose and power, trusting that with You, Lord, nothing is impossible. Embrace me as I seek You this day, for yours is the Kingdom that never dies and the love that never ends.

All the believers devoted themselves to the apostles' teaching, and to fellowship, and to sharing in meals (including the Lord's Supper), and to prayer.
A deep sense of awe came over them all, and the apostles performed many miraculous signs and wonders. And all the believers met together in one place and shared everything they had. They sold their property and possessions and shared the money with those in need. They worshiped together at the Temple each day, met in homes for the Lord's Supper, and shared their meals with great joy and generosity—all the while praising God and enjoying the goodwill of all the people. And each day the Lord added to their fellowship those who were being saved. Acts 2:42-47 (NLT)

I can serve God today by . . .

JUNE 12

O Lord of the Sabbath, as I rest in your presence, I realize that Sundays come and go; I come to worship and find encouragement, hope, and clarity for my life—and I leave with good intentions. Yet often, when Monday morning comes, I find myself swept up in what feels like the whirling dervish of my day-to-day life. This week, help me to open my heart so that I might discover the obstacles that prevent me from living the life You so desire for me. Clear away the self-serving in my prayers and my thoughts. Help me to see what You see in me. Pull me out of my own denial and grant me the wide-angled lens to see the panorama of life through your eyes. And then, O Lord, remind me why I am here on this earth—to love You and to love those You have entrusted to me.

I have pointed you in the way of wisdom;
    I have steered you down the path to integrity.
So get going. And as you go, *know this: with integrity* you will overcome all obstacles;
    even if you run, you will not stumble.
Proverbs 4:11-12 (The Voice)

What are my obstacles to spiritual growth?

JUNE 13

Comforting God, be near to all whose names I whisper in my heart now. Expand my heart to embrace the burdens of others so that I may offer calm assurance to those who worry and soothing words to those who are in pain. Awaken my spirit to the ones who are adept at hiding their burdens that I might walk beside them, simply offering the gift of presence. Expand my capacity to care so that You will create in me a sanctuary of grace that welcomes the poor in spirit.

"Am I a God who is only close at hand? says the LORD.
"No, I am far away at the same time.
Can anyone hide from me in a secret place?
Am I not everywhere in all the heavens and earth?"
says the LORD. Jeremiah 23:23-24 (NLT)

Black bear, Montana

Lord God, for all I sense and learn and experience, I thank You. For the gift of rest and renewal, for the ebb and flow of each season, for discoveries and delights, I praise You. During the sleepy times of summer, help me to take some time to relax under the canopy of your holy presence. Deliver me from my never-ending pursuit of the urgent, and instead, re-orient me to what is truly important in my life. Help me to create space for your Word to break through—to create time to be still, to pray, to listen, to rejoice.

Truly my soul finds rest in God;
  my salvation comes from him.
Truly he is my rock and my salvation;
  he is my fortress, I will never be shaken.
Psalm 62:1-2 (NIV)

In what way do I need to learn to rest?

O God of calming presence, You have reminded me of my need to center my soul deeply in a place of trust in You. Free me from my restless worries and my preoccupation with what I cannot control, for You have invited me to be still and dwell in You without fear, to simply rest and trust. Lord, as You once spoke peace to the wind and the waves, whisper your calm over my heart so that I might wait silently and learn to enjoy the gift of your companionship. And then begin your life-changing work, taking me from fearful to confident and from shaken to courageous as I walk with You.

You know what I am going to say
*   even before I say it, LORD.*
You go before me and follow me.
*   You place your hand of blessing on my head.*
Such knowledge is too wonderful for me,
*   too great for me to understand!*
Psalm 139:4-6 (NLT)

I feel calm when . . .

JUNE 16

Lord of light, help me to immerse myself not just in the world around me but also in the experience of your beauty and grace living within my soul. Help me not only to feel the light of Jesus Christ deep within my heart but also to allow that light to expand. Open my eyes to see the path that You are lighting before me, the path that Jesus walked before me. Help me to trust You boldly and walk in your way so that my life might truly be a reflection of living in your Kingdom right here on earth.

Thy word is a lamp unto my feet, and a light unto my path. Psalm 119:105 King James Version (KJV)

Newport, Oregon

For the next ten minutes, ask yourself, "What would help me connect with God right now?"

Gracious God, I am yearning for something more than the superficial life for which I so easily settle. You have planted within me the appetite for life in all its fullness, which is rooted and grounded in your grace. Sometimes I feel like a newcomer on this journey, not knowing exactly where to begin. Yet, You reach out to me, asking me to simply knock on the door, to call out for your Presence, for You have promised to meet me in my seeking.

For I know the plans I have for you, declares the LORD, *plans to prosper you and not to harm you, plans to give you hope and a future. Then you will call on me and come and pray to me, and I will listen to you. You will seek me and find me when you seek me with all your heart.* Jeremiah 29:11-13 (NIV)

I trust God's plan for my . . .

Yahweh, Lord of the universe, too often I find myself rattled, unsettled, and shaken by life's battles; yet I know that entering into prayer takes me into the calm of your presence. Indeed, within my soul You dwell as the center of a perfect and abiding peace. My confidence in your strength emerges from the knowledge that You are constantly with me. I know that You care enough to hear the whispered stirrings of my heart.

"Go out and stand before me on the mountain," the LORD told him. And as Elijah stood there, the LORD passed by, and a mighty windstorm hit the mountain. It was such a terrible blast that the rocks were torn loose, but the LORD was not in the wind. After the wind there was an earthquake, but the LORD was not in the earthquake. And after the earthquake there was a fire, but the LORD was not in the fire. And after the fire there was the sound of a gentle whisper. 1 Kings 19:11-12 (NLT)

I whisper to God about . . .

Loving God, on this Father's Day I am especially grateful for the gift of family. I pray that You will bless fathers with the gift of courage so that they might be able to withstand life's challenges. Give them a shield of faith that will lead them to strengthen their foundation in You. Instill in them the light of hope to sustain them through each of life's trials.

Many of us are reminded of the fathers who are no longer with us, and we ask for your presence in those recollections. We give thanks for their loving legacies; where we need healing, offer to us the grace of letting go in trust.

O Lord, I pray that You will empower all fathers so that You might use their lives as a testimony to your great grace at work in ordinary lives.

Honor your father and your mother, so that you may live long in the land the LORD your God is giving you. Exodus 20:12 (NIV)

Jonesport, Maine

JUNE 20

Shepherd of my soul, You are the ever-open door. Your grace reaches out to embrace me even before I know I am seeking. Open my spirit to hear your call— that still, small voice that touches the center of my being—to be the person You created me to be. You invite me to forgiveness even before my heart is ready to repent. Help me to be receptive to the sometimes comforting, sometimes challenging, often surprising ways You communicate with me. Then help me to take just one more step with You, Lord.

You have searched me, *LORD*,
   and you know me.
You know when I sit and when I rise;
   you perceive my thoughts from afar.
You discern my going out and my lying down;
   you are familiar with all my ways.
Psalm 139:1-3 (NIV)

God challenges me to . . .

O Lord who sojourns with me daily, I surrender to You the frightened and uncertain places in my heart, the places within me that ring with questions, the parts that are pounded by doubts. I offer to You both the words of my mouth and the sighs of my heart. You loosen the knots of confusion, discouragement, and need in my life. In those moments, You surprise me with your presence, reminding me once again that despite my fears, I never walk alone.

For he will command his angels concerning you
   to guard you in all your ways;
they will lift you up in their hands
   so that you will not strike your foot against a stone.
Psalm 91:11-12 (NIV)

Which quandary needs God's wisdom?

JUNE 22

O Lord of these summer days, your beauty is stamped on all of creation. Your presence is around me in a thousand wonders, from the zigzag flash of lightning, to the smallest raindrop; from the expanse of the ocean, to tiny, darting tropical fish. I can descend into the depths of the ocean or ascend into the midnight blue of the star-studded night sky and sense your glory all around me. And here, in this time of prayer, I sense the unmistakable touch of your Spirit within me. Lord, You are a wondrous, almighty God.

Honor the LORD for the glory of his name.
   Worship the LORD in the splendor of his holiness.
The voice of the LORD echoes above the sea.
   The God of glory thunders.
   The LORD thunders over the mighty sea.
Psalm 29:2-3 (NLT)

Anenome, British Columbia

O wondrous God, thank you for all the blessings of life and for answers to many prayers—prayers answered that I didn't even realize I prayed, prayers not answered that turned out to be blessings. Thank you for the people who remind me of what is important in this life: friends who are faithful and people I can count on when I am stretched beyond my limits. I offer You the prayers of my heart, trusting You will be at work in each situation, bringing goodness out of life's difficulties.

Sing for joy, O heavens, and exult, O earth;
  break forth, O mountains, into singing!
For the LORD has comforted his people,
  and will have compassion on his suffering ones.
Isaiah 49:13 (NSRV)

The prayers of my heart are . . .

JUNE 24

You call out to me, Lord, with the gift of solitude so that I might step back from the turbulence of the times to reflect on the direction of my life. I want to trust that You love me as I am, but I waver in my willingness to follow You. Your Spirit reveals to me my weaknesses and my shortcomings, yet You promise fresh beginnings in each new moment. Show me daily how to walk with Jesus and to honor you.

So here's what I want you to do, God helping you: Take your everyday, ordinary life—your sleeping, eating, going-to-work, and walking-around life—and place it before God as an offering. Embracing what God does for you is the best thing you can do for him. Don't become so well-adjusted to your culture that you fit into it without even thinking. Instead, fix your attention on God. You'll be changed from the inside out. Readily recognize what he wants from you, and quickly respond to it. Unlike the culture around you, always dragging you down to its level of immaturity, God brings the best out of you, develops well-formed maturity in you. Romans 12:1-2 (The Message)

When I reflect on the direction of my life, I realize that . . .

JUNE 25

Bountiful God, today I am especially grateful for the promise of the changing rhythms of summertime—for longer days that linger into twilight, for road trips and family gatherings, for weekends away and walks along the beach. I am also thankful for the changing rhythms of my soul as I find myself slowing down just a little and breathing more deeply, experiencing the delight of gardens aflame with glorious color. For all these wonders that make my spirits soar, I give You praise.

The flowers appear on the earth;
*   the time of singing has come,*
and the voice of the turtledove
*   is heard in our land.*
Song of Solomon 2:12 (NRSV)

Camden, Maine

JUNE 26

Merciful God, thank you for offering your Shepherd's heart to each person: to the frail, You offer comfort; to the mourning, a glimpse of joy; to the self-sufficient, a reminder of vulnerability; to the seeking, abundant hope. You are relentless in seeking me, inviting me back to You, and then inspiring me to live a life reflecting your Son, Jesus.

Come, let us worship and bow down.
Let us kneel before the LORD our maker,
for he is our God.
We are the people he watches over,
the flock under his care.
If only you would listen to his voice today!
Psalm 95:6-7 (NLT)

How could I live more selflessly?

JUNE 27

Gentle One, I have to admit that at times in my life, despair feels crushing, and fear leaves me brittle. In those moments, I ask that You would keep me from reacting with too much haste or speaking words that I will regret later. O Lord, in those instants, I know I am not thinking clearly, so I ask for your steadying presence that I might rest in your peace and respond with patience, waiting for your vision to show me a way forward in faith.

One who is slow to anger is better than the mighty,
  and one whose temper is controlled than one who captures a city.
Proverbs 16:32 (NRSV)

I need patience to . . .

JUNE 28

O Lord of this new day, whose majesty bursts the bounds of creation, your glory is ever-present in the canopy of billowing clouds in the skies above and in the verdant greens of the land below. You have sprinkled vibrant flowers over the meadows to dazzle my senses. Your blessings are scattered with abandon all around me, yet I ask You once again to give me the spiritual eyes to see your hand at work all around me each and every day.

May the God of your father help you;
*   may the Almighty bless you*
with the blessings of the heavens above,
*   and blessings of the watery depths below, . . .*
Genesis 49:25a (NLT)

West River, Vermont

> Pastor Tim Keller wisely offered these words about God answering our prayers: "God says: 'When a child of mine makes a request, I always give them what they would have asked for if they knew everything I know.' "

Compassionate God, when I find myself in trouble, when I reach the end of my limited resources, I know I need your guidance. Help me to humble myself to simply ask and then release the problem into your tender care. Remind me of this basic truth—if I surrender my troubles to You, You will fill me again with the strength I need.

O LORD, God of my salvation,
when, at night, I cry out in your presence,
let my prayer come before you;
incline your ear to my cry.
Psalm 88:1-2 (NRSV)

What needs do I want to offer to God in prayer?

JUNE 30

Lord of the universe whose Spirit lives within me, I ask that You would release me from my own restricted world view. Save me from my single-minded focus in difficulties. Re-orient my mind so that I might see each one as an opportunity for growth. Help me not to settle for a limited life, but through your power, to live the life You have planned for me.

Before you know it, the Spirit of GOD will come on you and you'll be prophesying right along with them. And you'll be transformed. You'll be a new person!
When these confirming signs are accomplished, you'll know that you're ready: Whatever job you're given to do, do it. God is with you!
1 Samuel 10:6-7 (The Message)

Where are the opportunities for growth in my life?

Half Dome, Yosemite National Park, CA

JULY 3

O God of this day and all moments in time, I surrender my swirling thoughts in gratitude to You. When spontaneous laughter bubbles up, I see your hand and give thanks. Imagining children splashing in a leaping fountain, I glimpse your glory. When an unexpected kindness breaks into my emptiness, your graciousness takes me by surprise. Even in the deepest challenges of my life, I can look back and see your presence giving strength and comfort. O God of my heart, You appear in the most ordinary moments of life, and I am humbled by a love that is unlike anything I have ever known. For that I am eternally grateful.

. . . The joy of GOD is your strength! Nehemiah 8:10b (The Message)

I feel God's love when I . . .

JULY 4

O Lord, on this festive day when starbursts of fireworks will illuminate the sky, I am so grateful for all the freedoms I treasure, especially the freedom to worship You.

Now I pray that I would know the power of your presence through word and prayer and laughter and song. Teach me the art of listening much more than I speak, perceiving your hidden hand, and showing me daily how to love with generosity of heart.

But whenever someone turns to the Lord, the veil is taken away. For the Lord is the Spirit, and wherever the Spirit of the Lord is, there is freedom. So all of us who have had that veil removed can see and reflect the glory of the Lord. And the Lord—who is the Spirit—makes us more and more like him as we are changed into his glorious image. 2 Corinthians 3:16-18 (NLT)

Danby, Vermont

JULY 1

Almighty God, when I am immersed in a jumble of daily activities, remind me that You are my center. When I become overwhelmed by worry, remind me that You are the Lord of all circumstances. When I become discouraged because of the many mountains before me, remind me that You are my mountain mover. As I pray, I reach out to You, O God, knowing that You have already enfolded me in your arms.

But me he caught—reached all the way
from sky to sea; he pulled me out
Of that ocean of hate, that enemy chaos,
the void in which I was drowning.
They hit me when I was down,
but GOD stuck by me.
He stood me up on a wide-open field;
I stood there saved—surprised to be loved!
Psalm 18:16-19 (The Message)

JULY 2

God of grace, I enter these moments of quiet prayer, grateful for the promise of your peace that gently reminds me that You are with me always. I cling to the words of my Lord Jesus, "Come to me all who are weary and heavy laden and I will give you rest." As I move into this week, enable me to carry that promise as You bring it to mind in moments throughout the day. Lead me to seek You when I feel worn, burnt out, and bent over with exhaustion, trusting that You will teach me the renewal that can come only from abiding in You.

So let's not allow ourselves to get fatigued doing good. At the right time we will harvest a good crop if we don't give up, or quit. Right now, therefore, every time we get the chance, let us work for the benefit of all, starting with the people closest to us in the community of faith. Galatians 6:9-10 (The Message)

When I am tired, I can seek God by . . .

JULY 5

"Prayer is not asking. Prayer is putting oneself in the hands of God, at His disposition, and listening to His voice in the depth of our hearts." (Mother Teresa)

O God of all life, whose hand molded me delicately, You created me from the inside out; You sculpted me from nothing into something; and as hard as it is for me to comprehend, You treasure me as your cherished child. So Lord, once again I am in your presence with my voice stilled but mind still humming with images and thoughts and plans. Help me to let go of the clutter of my thoughts and be still, so that I might enter the peace in which You dwell. Enable me not only to glimpse the holy in the commonplace but to glory in You and praise You, the Creator of it all.

You made all the delicate, inner parts of my body
and knit me together in my mother's womb.
Thank you for making me so wonderfully complex!
Your workmanship is marvelous—how well I know it.
You watched me as I was being formed in utter seclusion,
as I was woven together in the dark of the womb.
You saw me before I was born.
Every day of my life was recorded in your book.
Every moment was laid out
before a single day had passed.
Psalm 139:13-16 (NLT)

I want to let go of . . .

JULY 6

Merciful God, I kneel in prayer, asking You to bring peace to those I see every day who are struggling: friends who are facing the sting of loss; loved ones who feel the dark cloud of discouragement; families who worry about loved ones' illnesses; others who come to You with deeply personal needs. May the power of your Holy Spirit empower and heal each one whose name I lift to You in prayer. Help me to live your Word in every breath so that others might see Christ in me. Help me to be your message—to love.

Jesus traveled throughout the region of Galilee, teaching in the synagogues and announcing the Good News about the Kingdom. And he healed every kind of disease and illness. Matthew 4:23 (NLT)

Which loved ones need my prayers today?

JULY 7

Lord of these mellow days, help me to take some time to relax under the umbrella of your holy presence. Deliver me from my never-ending hurry sickness and remind me of what is significant in my life—and what is significant to You. Help me to make space for You, to create time to be still, to pray, to listen, to rejoice. O Lord, I yearn to feel your unmistakable presence in the midst of all that clutters my life and then to sense You calming my spirit.

I will sing to the LORD all my life;
   I will sing praise to my God as I live.
May my meditation be pleasing to him,
   as I rejoice in the LORD.
Psalm 104:33-34 (NIV)

Water lily, Vermont

JULY 8

O God, You are the Author of all possibility, the Novelist of new beginnings, and the Builder of hope-filled futures. In this brand new day, I ask You to step in and be at work in every situation I encounter. Breathe new hope and inspiration into my life and keep me ever mindful that I am more than a conqueror through the One who loves me, Jesus, my Lord.

No, in all these things we are more than conquerors through him who loved us. For I am convinced that neither death nor life, neither angels nor demons, neither the present nor the future, nor any powers, neither height nor depth, nor anything else in all creation, will be able to separate us from the love of God that is in Christ Jesus our Lord. Romans 8:37-39 (NIV)

Where in my life do I need a new beginning?

JULY 9

Precious Lord, your very nature is to be present with me through both the joyful times of my life and the painful ones. Thank you for that deep sense of need within me that keeps me ever-longing for You. Open my heart and mind to your presence today. Sometimes I rejoice over the wonderful, amazing blessings that You are giving to me and those I love. But today my heart hopes for healing for my wounded spirit. I bring before You my hurt, conflicts, and worries, even my anger and broken relationships. O Lord, receive me as I ask for the desire to be in a whole relationship with You and with others. Forgive me, heal my wayward ways, and enable me to begin again.

"My wayward children," says the LORD,
  "come back to me, and I will heal your wayward hearts."
"Yes, we're coming," the people reply,
  "for you are the LORD our God."
Jeremiah 3:22 (NLT)

Lord, I need healing for . . .

JULY 10

O God who gifted me with the treasure of Sabbath peace, You have led me to begin this day with a leisurely sense of your presence. Just for today, help me to discover the joy of doing "serious nothing"—porch rocking, hammock swinging, laughing with friends, and resting in You—so that I might become aware of the precious beauty of the gift of this life You have given me. Lead me to live this day in the unhurried rhythms of your grace.

By entering through faith into what God has always wanted to do for us—set us right with him, make us fit for him—we have it all together with God because of our Master Jesus. And that's not all: We throw open our doors to God and discover at the same moment that he has already thrown open his door to us. We find ourselves standing where we always hoped we might stand—out in the wide open spaces of God's grace and glory, standing tall and shouting our praise. Romans 5:1-2 (The Message)

Camden, Maine

JULY 11

O God of creation, it only takes is a moment of being fully alive to awaken to your glory all around me. The season's zephyr winds soothe my weary spirit. The shifting shapes in the clouds delight the child within me. The birds gliding effortlessly remind me that You sustain my every breath. I have discovered that some seasons in life seem to radiate beauty and joy; yet in others I feel troubled by clouds of dreary grayness. I admit that I would much rather live in the joys of discipleship and skip the challenges that come with following You in my world. It is in those times that You remind me that in my world I will have tribulation, but ultimately You will overcome any darkness I might encounter with the light of your Son, Jesus.

Jesus answered them, "Do you now believe? Behold, the hour is coming, indeed it has come, when you will be scattered, each to his own home, and will leave me alone. Yet I am not alone, for the Father is with me. I have said these things to you, that in me you may have peace. In the world you will have tribulation. But take heart; I have overcome the world." John 16:31-33 (ESV)

What is God calling me to do in this season of my life?

JULY 12

Both of my daughters' favorite children's book was *Anne of Green Gables*, and we watched the DVD more times that you can imagine. We repeated one line over and over: "Every day is fresh, with no mistakes in it yet." This is good theology.

Dear Lord, thank you for being a God who invites me to come to You as I am, without fear. I am so grateful for your meeting my tiny bit of faith with your steadfast love and mercy. I do ask You to forgive my doubting when I am afraid to trust your goodness. Draw me into your love this day as I take steps of faith into the embrace of your grace.

I cried out, "I am slipping!"
   but your unfailing love, O LORD, supported me.
When doubts filled my mind,
   your comfort gave me renewed hope and cheer.
Psalm 94:18-19 (NLT)

What are my honest spiritual doubts?

JULY 13

Heavenly God, help me to experience your beauty and grace through the Holy Spirit who reminds me of your presence abiding within me. Help me to know your light deep within so that my life might truly be a reflection of You. Open my eyes to see the path that You are lighting before me—the path that Jesus walked long ago so that I might trust You boldly, walking in His way.

My child, listen and be wise:
  Keep your heart on the right course.
Proverbs 23:19 (NLT)

Pacific Rim National Park, Canada

JULY 14

Loving Lord, thank you for every touch of healing peace and strengthening hope that You have given me this week. My heart overflows with gratitude as I recognize your invitation to come into your presence, bringing all that I am, all my dreams and my hopes, all my faith and my doubts. Dear God, re-orient my life by the compass of your Holy Spirit. Hear my growing desire for You to be at the center of my life. Search my heart, O Lord, seek me out, sift my motives, and set me on your right path as I follow in the steps of Jesus.

Search me, God, and know my heart;
*   test me and know my anxious thoughts.*
See if there is any offensive way in me,
*   and lead me in the way everlasting.*
Psalm 139:23-24 (NIV)

My hopes and dreams include . . .

JULY 15

O God of hope, scenes of unbearable tragedy and devastation have buffeted my senses. I pray for comfort and healing for each one who has been affected: those who are grieving for family members who have perished; the ones barely surviving without life's basic necessities, water, food, and a place to call home; those who are dealing with the uncertainty of simply not knowing if their loved ones are safe. I know that You are the one who provides both comfort and hope. Lead me to reach out as the hands and feet of Christ in my world. Let your love so blaze in my life that it might spark joy and hope all around me.

Then the King will say to those on his right, "Come, you who are blessed by my Father; take your inheritance, the kingdom prepared for you since the creation of the world. For I was hungry and you gave me something to eat, I was thirsty and you gave me something to drink, I was a stranger and you invited me in, I needed clothes and you clothed me, I was sick and you looked after me, I was in prison and you came to visit me."
Then the righteous will answer him, "Lord, when did we see you hungry and feed you, or thirsty and give you something to drink? When did we see you a stranger and invite you in, or needing clothes and clothe you? When did we see you sick or in prison and go to visit you?"
The King will reply, "Truly I tell you, whatever you did for one of the least of these brothers and sisters of mine, you did for me." Matthew 25:34-40 (NIV)

I could serve God today by . . .

JULY 16

Lord of this new morning, I feel your artistic majesty in the warmth of the summer breeze. The wind of your Spirit sweeps through my life—sometimes bringing with it the breeze of refreshment, sometimes carrying gusts that shift me off balance, and other times engulfing me in the whipping winds of life change. Yet, often that same wind reminds me of your constant presence sustaining me, and though I cannot see it, I know its presence all around me. When I let go, releasing my tight grip over the circumstances of my life, and rest in You, You help me to sail toward You with confident peace.

I lift up my eyes to the mountains—
*   where does my help come from?*
My help comes from the LORD,
*   the Maker of heaven and Earth.*
Psalm 121:1-2 (NIV)

Rockport, Maine

JULY 17

Loving Lord, thank you for every touch of healing peace and strengthening hope that You have given me this week. My heart overflows with gratitude as I recognize your invitation to come into your presence, bringing all that I am, all my dreams and my hopes, all my faith and my doubts. Dear God, re-orient my life by the compass of your Holy Spirit. Hear my growing desire for You to be at the center of my life. Search my heart, O Lord, seek me out, sift my motives, and set me on your right path as I follow in the steps of Jesus.

Search me, God, and know my heart;
*   test me and know my anxious thoughts.*
See if there is any offensive way in me,
*   and lead me in the way everlasting.*
Psalm 139:23-24 (NIV)

My hopes and dreams include . . .

JULY 18

O Lord of joy, your presence touches me like sunshine peeking through the clouds on a dark, stormy morning, shining your light of grace on me when I reach out to You. O God, You are eager for me to see the light of your glory dawning around me. Thank you for the gift of each new day, for it is the unmistakable sign of your presence, of your Kingdom unfolding on earth and in my heart.

The Sovereign LORD has given me his words of wisdom,
*   so that I know how to comfort the weary.*
Morning by morning he wakens me
*   and opens my understanding to his will.*
The Sovereign LORD has spoken to me,
*   and I have listened.*
*   I have not rebelled or turned away.*
Isaiah 50:4-5 (NLT)

With the gift of this day I can . . .

JULY 19

Glorious God, I praise You for eternal moments when I celebrate the gift of everyday epiphanies of grace—for a smile after a long sadness, for the heart-stopping hush when I glimpse a newborn foal in a meadow. But my eyes sometimes fail to see the sparkle of diamonds dancing across the waters or a butterfly's waltz through a spring garden. Everything seems somehow brighter when You are at the center of my thoughts and intentions. Thank you for granting me the vision to attend to creation's bounty as I live in timeless moments, praising You for it all.

. . . Instead be filled with the Spirit, speaking to one another with psalms, hymns, and songs from the Spirit. Sing and make music from your heart to the Lord, always giving thanks to God the Father for everything, in the name of our Lord Jesus Christ. Ephesians 5:18b-20 (NIV)

Versailles, Kentucky

I spent a lot of years in my prayer life talking at God. But recently I've started a different prayer practice: I have been asking God questions and then listening for a response. I don't often hear right away, but when I wait, God usually answers. My question has been, "What do You want me to let go of?" It might be a different question for you. But think about asking God a question in prayer.

Welcoming Lord, no matter where I have been, You still want me to seek You in prayer. So I enter this time of prayer with a sense of anticipation and hope that your presence will nourish, comfort, and encourage me. How grateful I am for your renewing power that meets me each day as I experience forgiveness, a freed spirit, and a grace-renewed life.

He lets me rest in green meadows;
*   he leads me beside peaceful streams.*
*   He renews my strength.*
He guides me along right paths,
*   bringing honor to his name.*
Psalm 23:2-3 (NLT)

When I listen for a response from God, I discover . . .

JULY 21

Dear God, when I am completely honest with myself, I recognize the ways I turn my back on You. I fill my life with "muchness" and busyness, crowding out the space in which I might sense your presence or hear your voice. Forgive me for putting the unimportant ahead of seeking You in my life. Open my spirit afresh so that I might choose differently in the day ahead.

What I'm trying to do here is get you to relax, not be so preoccupied with *getting* so you can respond to God's *giving*. People who don't know God and the way he works fuss over these things, but you know both God and how he works. Steep yourself in God-reality, God-initiative, God-provisions. You'll find all your everyday human concerns will be met. Don't be afraid of missing out. You're my dearest friends! The Father wants to give you the very kingdom itself. Luke 12:29-32 (The Message)

What is insignificant, yet clutters my life?

JULY 22

Thank you, O Comforting God, that You hear the prayer of my heart and the prayers of those I love:

    those who rejoice over children's simple delight;

    those who mourn at the end of life's circle;

    those who are grateful when their work meets with success;

    those who suffer because no work is to be found;

    those who are weary, having too much to do;

    those who are waiting and longing for love's touch.

Thank you for meeting me in every season of my life, providing everything I may need.

I love you, LORD;
   you are my strength.
The LORD is my rock, my fortress, and my savior;
   my God is my rock, in whom I find protection.
He is my shield, the power that saves me,
   and my place of safety.
Psalm 18:1-2 (NLT)

    Laurie Bohlke

JULY 23

Sign at a retreat center: "Welcome to this place of solitude. Please feel free to take off your masks." That is an invitation to us every moment as we seek God's nurturing presence in prayer.

Gracious God, You know me better than I know myself; You have looked in my heart and have seen the secrets and the successes, the doubtings and the yearnings. I surrender all of myself to You with an open heart. I sense a calling to a different way of living, to something more than this world can offer to me. You call me to come to You as I am and help me to see that You want to transform me from the inside out. And I often find myself confused and resistant. You invite me to release the parts of myself that keep me safe and stuck, the parts that I hide even from myself, my self-absorption and self-seeking ways. You offer me the way to spiritual growth, yet I so often shrink from the process. Grant me the vision and courage to trust that your will and your ways will lead me to abundant life in You.

He has told you, O mortal, what is good.
    And what does the LORD require of you?
To act justly and love mercy
    and to walk humbly with your God.
Micah 6:8 (NIV)

Give me the courage, Lord, to be open to . . .

JULY 24

God of the ages and God of this moment, I have sensed You drawing me closer. Sometimes You've reached out like a blaze of light in the midst of a dark night, yet often your touch has been much more subtle in ordinary moments that open my mind and spirit to growth. And much like the first disciples, when I have chosen to take the risk to respond, You have answered by reassuring me that You honor my courage. In a world that regularly shouts that I am not enough, I know my worth is in You. Lord of life, bless me in these days with a deeper trust in your ways.

Seek GOD, while he's here to be found,
pray to him while he's close at hand.
Let the wicked abandon their way of life
and the evil their way of thinking.
Let them come back to GOD, who is merciful,
come back to our GOD, who is lavish with forgiveness.
Isaiah 55:6-7 (The Message)

How has God been lavish to me?

JULY 25

Lord of these vacation days, I lift to You my morning prayers of praise. Under the warmth of this summer sunshine, the world awakens into a rainbow of color. You breathed this world into being, and your hand is discernable in every corner of it. I marvel at the harmony of nature, the smooth whorls of a solitary fingerprint, the expanse of a mountain meadow, and the Artist's vision that sculpted it all. So I gladly turn to You with gratitude overflowing from the wellspring of a joy-bursting heart.

I will praise you, LORD, with all my heart;
  I will tell of all the marvelous things you have done.
I will be filled with joy because of you.
  I will sing praises to your name, O Most High.
Psalm 9:1-2 (NLT)

Minturn, Colorado

JULY 26

Wonderful Counselor, Prince of Peace, sometimes my heart is filled with fearful questions. Where are You in the midst of my situation? How can I sense your presence? Can I trust You with the concerns of my heart? Whatever my swirling thoughts might be, I lift them into your hands with hopeful trust that You will meet me where I am today. Lord, open my heart and replace my doubts and fears with faith and peace.

They will have no fear of bad news;
*   their hearts are steadfast, trusting in the LORD.*
Their hearts are secure, they will have no fear; . . .
Psalm 112:7-8a (NIV)

What questions do I want to ask God today?

JULY 27

O Lord of all life, in whose image I have been fashioned, thank you that You have formed me as a unique creation. When I am tempted to think less of myself or others, remind me of the simple, profound truth that I am loved by You. Anchored in that awareness, lead me to orient my life toward the people whose lives intersect with mine. Grant me the grace I need to treat them with your merciful love and with truth tempered by your kindness.

And yet, O LORD, you are our Father.
   We are the clay, and you are the potter.
   We all are formed by your hand.
Isaiah 64:8 (NLT)

I need to offer God's grace to . . .

JULY 28

Wondrous God, when sunshine dances across the cornflower sky, your glory shines through the heavens. Today, I begin to count my blessings one by one, and my cup overflows. I praise You for the joy of freshly cut hay, for families reunited after a long absence, for hope stirred, and for faith renewed. O Lord, with each breath I take, I celebrate your gifts of abundant life.

From the dew of heaven
*   and the richness of the earth,*
may God always give you abundant harvests of grain
*   and bountiful new wine.*
Genesis 27:28 (NLT)

Danby, Vermont

JULY 29

I learned something at our Wednesday night class last week. Pastor John Ortberg wrote, "If you can worry, you can meditate." Worry is simply reverse meditation. Every time I find myself obsessing about what I cannot control or focusing on the negative, I have a choice: I can worry, or I can roll the goodness and the faithfulness and the trustworthiness of God over and over in my mind. I do have a choice.

All-knowing God, as I reflect on the people I meet each day, I recognize each person as unique, but I see only the surface—the smiles, the frowns, the sleepiness, the liveliness. I know that expressions can be misleading. Only You know what is churning beneath. I know that worries have a way of consuming my mind; fears hold me back; resentments separate me from others; criticism clouds my judgment; and sorrows press me down. Whatever lies beneath the surface, I pray for your Holy Spirit to touch me with wisdom.

Who is wise and understanding among you? Let them show it by their good life, by deeds done in the humility that comes from wisdom.
James 3:13 (NIV)

Beneath the surface I am wrestling with . . .

JULY 30

Loving Lord, I am grateful for those moments when You have found me stumbling in all the wrong places, and You did not treat me as lost. Instead, You welcomed me as a cherished one joyously found. Thank you for the gift of forgiveness in the face of my great carelessness with your grace. You have poured out your Spirit in my life and gently summoned me to once again follow You.

And all of this is a gift from God, who brought us back to himself through Christ. And God has given us this task of reconciling people to him. For God was in Christ, reconciling the world to himself, no longer counting people's sins against them. And he gave us this wonderful message of reconciliation. So we are Christ's ambassadors; God is making his appeal through us. We speak for Christ when we plead, "Come back to God!" 2 Corinthians 5:18-20 (NLT)

I want to follow Jesus so that I can . . .

JULY 31

O God of grace, I come before You this morning in anticipation, hoping that if I can find a way to open my heart, You will meet me here. If I can find the courage to risk being honest, your presence will fill me to overflowing. And so I pray and I wait. I need your help, O Lord, because on my own, my mind races, my heart hardens, my spirit becomes self-sufficient, and I miss out on the wondrous opportunities that You offer in all of my ordinary moments. Soften my heart, Lord, and hear my prayer.

"The LORD is my portion," says my soul,
  "therefore I will hope in him."
The LORD is good to those who wait for him,
  to the soul who seeks him.
It is good that one should wait quietly
  for the salvation of the LORD.
Lamentations 3: 24-26 (ESV)

Mountain lion, Montana

AUGUST 1

O Lord of stunning beauty, I am grateful this morning for summertime: for days of leisure that allow me to retreat from the work world simply to enjoy the gift of the ordinary—for the chance to capture children's exuberant spirits as they run with abandon and for the opportunity to be quiet enough to compose in my mind a new gratitude list of your blessings to me. You remind me, moment by moment, that life in Jesus is a gift to be enjoyed and celebrated daily. You sow the seeds of life within the hearts of each one willing to trust You. In You, I find a new way to live and a renewed spirit to offer others.

What a God we have! And how fortunate we are to have him, this Father of our Master Jesus! Because Jesus was raised from the dead, we've been given a brand-new life and have everything to live for, including a future in heaven— and the future starts now! God is keeping careful watch over us and the future. The Day is coming when you'll have it all—life healed and whole.
1 Peter 1:3-5 (The Message)

Cape Cod, Massachusetts

AUGUST 2

Dear Lord, I give myself to your work in my life, as You remake me from weary to refreshed, from wounded to healed, from chained to forgiven, and from suffering to hope-filled. I trust once again that You will fill my life with purpose and laughter as I celebrate your presence. Empower me with courage and joy for each day so that I may offer strength and peace to others and to my world, in the name of Jesus Christ.

Mercy, peace and love be yours in abundance. Jude 1:2 (NIV)

What could I offer to others today?

Most Holy God, I know that my spirituality is incomplete if I cannot move from "me" to "we". So, my prayers reach outward to those who need your word: those whose resentment is simmering and forgiveness seems impossible; those who are beginning to understand that their compulsive behaviors have become unmanageable; and those who long to believe in You but struggle with being able to take the step of trusting.

As I name them one by one in a moment of silence, I ask You to be at work in ways I can't even imagine. Lord, I commend them to your care.

I am the good shepherd; I know my own sheep, and they know me, just as my Father knows me and I know the Father. So I sacrifice my life for the sheep. I have other sheep, too, that are not in this sheepfold. I must bring them also. They will listen to my voice, and there will be one flock with one shepherd.
John 10:14-16 (NLT)

Today I am naming these people in prayer . . .

AUGUST 4

Inviting Lord, thank you for the morning splendor that streams through my soul. Thank you for the sun's brilliance reflecting the breathtaking mountain vista before me, telling my heart that a new day has come. It is mine to use as one more opportunity in which to serve You, the Lord of earth and sky.

Awake, my soul!
  Awake, harp and lyre!
  I will awaken the dawn.
I will praise you, Lord, among the nations;
  I will sing of you among the peoples.
For great is your love, reaching to the heavens;
  your faithfulness reaches to the skies.
Psalm 57:8-10 (NIV)

Mt. Mansfield, Vermont

AUGUST 5

Blessed Lord, You remind me often that life is more than worrying about my own life—it is reaching out to others with the grace You have offered to me. This day give me the courage to speak a word of grace when it may not be easy to speak; help me to be a listening ear when I am tempted to give easy advice; and help me to reach out with a secret act of service that will never be discovered—in a word, help me to walk in the way of the Master this day. I pray in the name of the One who showed me a life built and sustained by prayer, Jesus the Christ.

What good is it, my brothers and sisters, if someone claims to have faith but has no deeds? Can such faith save them? Suppose a brother or a sister is without clothes and daily food. If one of you says to them, "Go in peace; keep warm and well fed," but does nothing about their physical needs, what good is it? In the same way, faith by itself, if it is not accompanied by action, is dead. James 2:14-17 (NIV)

To walk with Jesus, today I could . . .

AUGUST 6

O Healing God, bring wholeness to the ragged parts of my life. As much as I wish it were not so, I have come to realize that adversity has been one of my greatest teachers. Empower me to fully surrender my demands so that I might be free enough to see You at work in my challenges. Grant me the gift of your peace-filled presence today as I come to You in prayer.

This is what the Sovereign LORD, the Holy One of Israel, says:
"In repentance and rest is your salvation,
in quietness and trust is your strength,
but you would have none of it". . .
Yet the LORD longs to be gracious to you;
therefore he will rise up to show you compassion.
For the LORD is a God of justice.
Blessed are all who wait for him!
Isaiah 30:15,18 (NIV)

My challenges are . . .

AUGUST 7

To pray is to breathe. When I breathe deeply, I find that I am filled with life. Did you know that the Greek word *pneuma* in Scripture can be translated both Spirit, and breath?

O Lord of all, your glory fills the air. The brilliance of a meteor shower or the carpet of garden flowers or a tiny hummingbird hovering over a blossom sometimes stops me in my tracks and invites me to whisper, "O Lord, how great Thou art." I am filled with gratitude for prayers answered in a heartbeat or even after a long delay, for love renewed, for hope restored, for faith given wings. It is in moments like these that I pause before your glory and breathe in and out to repeat my everyday prayers of praise.

The Spirit of God has made me,
  and the breath of the Almighty gives me life.
Job 33:4 (ESV)

Hermit hummingbird, Ecuador   Jeff Wendorff

AUGUST 8

God of abundant life, on this bright morning, I praise You for moments of quiet joy—for a monarch butterfly pausing over a blossoming fire bush, for two squirrels playing a noisy game of tag, for baby ducklings following their mother in a tidy line. Wherever I turn, I glimpse reflections of your goodness.

Yet, my thoughts are often anywhere but on the present moment. I admit I seem to spend too much of my life hurrying and worrying, then live with knotted shoulders and tension headaches. I settle for a life consumed with thoughts about what might be instead of focusing on your faithfulness. Remind me always that tomorrow will take care of itself and that the Kingdom life You offer begins now. You have reminded me that You are the God of "I am"—You are the One who is with me in this very hour.

It is for freedom that Christ has set us free. Stand firm, then, and do not let yourselves be burdened again by a yoke of slavery. Galatians 5:1 (NIV)

I experienced a moment of quiet joy when . . .

Gracious God, I say that I am open to being transformed in your image, moving from entrenched patterns to new possibilities, from habits that have enslaved me to ones that enrich me, from self-absorption to a heart wide-open. Yet, settled in what seems comfortable and familiar, I often hesitate to take that plunge out of the boat, trusting that You will meet me there. Grant me the grace to be receptive enough to the changes You want to work in me, trusting You to lead me on the path of discipleship through my fears as I take steps of faith to choose and face a new future.

Shortly before dawn Jesus went out to them, walking on the lake. When the disciples saw him walking on the lake, they were terrified. "It's a ghost," they said, and cried out in fear.
But Jesus immediately said to them: "Take courage! It is I. Don't be afraid."
"Lord, if it's you," Peter replied, "tell me to come to you on the water."
"Come," he said.
Then Peter got down out of the boat, walked on the water and came toward Jesus. But when he saw the wind, he was afraid and, beginning to sink, cried out, "Lord, save me!"
Immediately Jesus reached out his hand and caught him. "You of little faith,"
he said, "why did you doubt?" Matthew 14:25-31 (NIV)

Where is God inviting me to plunge into the unknown?

AUGUST 10

Help me, O God, in these hot sultry days, to find moments to turn to You. Your presence touches me like sunshine on a stormy afternoon, shining your light on my life and on the countless others who reach out to You. Cut through the swirling clouds of my crowded life. Refresh me with the gentle rain of your Holy Spirit. Like a rumble of thunder and a bolt of lightning, startle me with new opportunities to serve You. I know that You are closer to me than the wind's whisper. Help me to be aware of your presence, to hear your voice and to recognize your Word speaking to me.

Listen, GOD, I'm calling at the top of my lungs:
   "Be good to me! Answer me!"
When my heart whispered, "Seek God,"
   my whole being replied,
"I'm seeking him!"
Psalm 27:7-8 (The Message)

Tioga Pass, California

Lord Jesus Christ, your Word teaches me that You prayed to meet the demands of your days on earth. You reached out to your Father at every juncture of life, including countless times when You could have chosen an easier way. You have taught me to seek your will and your ways so that I might know the joys of a life centered in You. Help me feel the power of your presence, through music and Word and silence. I know your Spirit abides in me every moment of every day. Lord, help me remember to reach out and seek your counsel, drawing wisdom from the power of your Spirit who is always at work within me.

I will sing of the LORD's great love forever;
  with my mouth I will make your faithfulness known
  through all generations.
Psalm 89:1 (NIV)

Are the joys of my life centered in You?

AUGUST 12

Dear Lord, in this season of recreation, whether I walk barefoot on the beach or stand gazing at a mountain peak or lie back in awe of the countless stars overhead, remind me that You remain the God of joy and laughter, and You are my God of re-creation.

God's glory is on tour in the skies,
  God-craft on exhibit across the horizon.
Madame Day holds classes every morning,
  Professor Night lectures each evening.
Their words aren't heard,
  their voices aren't recorded,
But their silence fills the earth:
  unspoken truth is spoken everywhere.
Psalm 19:1-4a (The Message)

My favorite outdoor place to feel God's glory is . . .

AUGUST 13

O God of new beginnings, as I turn to You, I recognize the places in my life that cry out for change. Sometimes, emptiness signals a place that begs to be filled, and other times, restlessness hints at needed shifts. The choices that You place before me are as unique as I am. Whether I am walking on a path of weary uncertainty that blinds me to your direction, or experiencing a chapter of struggle that drags me into discouragement, I trust that You are the one who can carry me through any wilderness in my life. You can empower me to press on through the rocky paths that cause me to stumble. Ultimately, I trust that You are the one who grants me what I need to make it through each day. I invite You, O God, to form me with a character to reflect the legacy of my Lord, Jesus.

And my God will meet all your needs according to the riches of his glory in Christ Jesus. Philippians 4:19 (NIV)

Red-billed Gulls, New Zealand

AUGUST 14

Years ago, actor Gary Cooper was interviewed and asked his definition of happiness. He responded, "It's simple, only one word really. It's gratitude."

God of this new day, who watches over me with endless love and care, thank you for this journey of life and all the wonders that lie before me. Your glory shows up in a thousand explosions of color and light, in mountain meadows blanketed with wildflowers and in bubbling waterfalls shooting droplets into the sparkling sunlight. Gift me with the ability to live each day with expectancy, eager for the mysteries You will unwrap for me, grateful for the richness of life's tapestry. Day by day I proclaim in quiet praise—great is your faithfulness, O Lord.

Hallelujah!
You who serve GOD, praise GOD!
    Just to speak his name is praise!
Just to remember GOD is a blessing—
    now and tomorrow and always.
From east to west, from dawn to dusk,
    keep lifting all your praises to GOD!
Psalm 113:1-3 (The Message)

Today I am eager for . . .

AUGUST 15

O God of possibility, as I turn to You, I invite You to form me with the character that reflects the legacy of Jesus, my Lord. I know too well how often I postpone and even avoid your call on my life. I hear You invite me to take new steps of faith, and I respond that I am not ready. You call me to dare to dream, and I respond that I don't have what it takes. You ask me to reach out to others, and I respond that I just don't have enough time. O Lord, in this journey of faith, You call me to be more than I can be on my own. And then, You remind me that your grace is sufficient for all my needs, for your power flows most powerfully in my weakness.

Now faith is confidence in what we hope for and assurance about what we do not see. Hebrews 11:1 (NIV)

My weaknesses keep me from . . .

AUGUST 16

O Lord who brings fresh blessings with this windswept morning, I praise You. Splashed with color, the dawn trumpets your presence with every new day. I lift up my grateful heart for the beauty of this earth—for an abundance of bright, summer flowers, the humming buzz of honey bees, healing sheets of rain, and shells scattered on the beach—all inviting discovery. Open wide the window of my spirit and fill me with light.

The LORD will guide you always;
*   he will satisfy your needs in a sun-scorched land*
*   and will strengthen your frame.*
You will be like a well-watered garden,
*   like a spring whose waters never fail.*
Isaiah 58:11 (NIV)

Maine coast garden

AUGUST 17

A couple of years ago, author Leonard Sweet came to JupiterFIRST Church and taught the congregation a short mantra based on Philippians 4:4-7. I've been focusing on it this week: "anxious, nothing; prayerful, everything; thankful, anything . . . PEACE."

Eternal One, in your great mercy You have reached out to me, inviting me to open wide the door of my spirit to You. Yet, I am concerned about the changes You might call me to make. You are before me, beckoning me to trust You completely, asking me to clean out my internal clutter, and encouraging me to let go of obstacles in my spiritual journey. You are pruning the overgrown parts of my life, helping me to release the behaviors that no longer serve me or those I love so that I might grow to become my truest self. I want to sense the peace of your presence and the refreshment of your grace.

Do not be anxious about anything, but in every situation, by prayer and petition, with thanksgiving, present your requests to God. And the peace of God, which transcends all understanding, will guard your hearts and your minds in Christ Jesus. Philippians 4:6-7 (NIV)

What internal clutter can I clean out today?

AUGUST 18

God of tenderness, thank you for nurturing me completely. Awaken in me the ear of a listener that I would be attentive to the various ways You speak to me. Each day, teach me the joy that overflows from the depths of a grateful life. Then grant me a spirit of service, O Lord, so that I might be one who serves with genuine gladness. Fill me that I might give out of the overflow and guide me so that I might venture with courage for this journey with Jesus.

This is what the LORD Almighty said: "Administer true justice; show mercy and compassion to one another. Do not oppress the widow or the fatherless, the foreigner or the poor. Do not plot evil against each other."
Zechariah 7:9-10 (NIV)

Today when I listen to God . . .

AUGUST 19

O God of peace, I rejoice that the sunrise celebrates a daily resurrection,
a celebration over fear:

my fear over the impact of yesterday's regrets,

my fear of what will meet me today,

my fear of what tomorrow might bring.

Remind me that in all times and places, You are here with me, offering your
peace and comfort and hope.

Like a bird protecting its young, God will cover you with His feathers,

will protect you under His great wings;

His faithfulness will form a shield around you, a rock-solid wall *to protect you.*

Psalm 91:4 (The Voice)

Israel   Tisa Queen-Oldham

AUGUST 20

Recently, I was privileged to celebrate my mother's 84th birthday with all of my siblings and many of her grandchildren. We shared all of the ways she has impacted each of our lives. I told her that her greatest gift to me was that she always believed in my abilities and my potential. And I thanked her. Later, I was struck by how much more God believes in me—and in each one of us.

God of the past, present, and yet-to-be, seasons will pass and time will change, but your faithfulness toward me remains. I long for the gift of your vision, yet know how easily I fall out of step with your Spirit. Re-orient my path and open my eyes so that I might look for glimpses of eternity and even recognize You in the midst of the ordinariness of my life. I know that nothing can separate me from your love. As I meet the challenges of the week ahead, help me to stand on the promise of your faithfulness. Lord, transform my life more and more to reflect the peace and joy I know as I place my trust in Jesus Christ, my Lord.

Because of Christ and our faith in him, we can now come boldly and confidently into God's presence. Ephesians 3:12 (NLT)

I have the potential to . . .

God of all compassion, in this sacred place I am reminded anew of the power of a community's prayers. I lift up those yearning for healing but who struggle with seemingly unanswered prayers. I pray for those who are burdened with chronic emotional or physical pain; for those whose fears have become a roadblock to faith; and for those who are filled with questions or anger or hurt. It is my prayer that, even in the darkness of the journey, You will embrace them and renew them with your presence. For it is in the challenging moments of life that You are cultivating in each of us the character of Jesus. It is always in Him that we are sustained.

Consider it a sheer gift, friends, when tests and challenges come at you from all sides. You know that under pressure, your faith-life is forced into the open and shows its true colors. So don't try to get out of anything prematurely. Let it do its work so you become mature and well-developed, not deficient in any way. James 1:2-4 (The Message)

Today my prayers for others include . . .

AUGUST 22

God of all blessings, Source of all life, Giver of all grace, I pause to give thanks—for the warmth of the blazing sun, for joyful vacation memories, for the comfort of old friends, for the anticipation of new beginnings, and most of all, for your grace that helps me become more than I could dream or imagine. I am humbled beyond measure by your abundant blessings.

And God raised us up with Christ and seated us with him in the heavenly realms in Christ Jesus, in order that in the coming ages he might show the incomparable riches of his grace, expressed in his kindness to us in Christ Jesus.
Ephesians 2:6-7 (NIV)

Marginal Way, Ogunquit, Maine

AUGUST 23

All-knowing God, You hear my sigh when I reach out to You. It is no accident that I have found myself here in this place this morning. The embrace of your Holy Spirit reaches out to wherever I might have been this week and wherever I might be in this moment. O Lord, I seek You, and over and over, You are the One who reaches out to me. You capture my attention in a chance word in a casual conversation, a memory from the past, the words of a song that speaks to my heart, a sentence that jumps out from a book, or an inner prompting that leads me to reach for You. When my spirit is open, I am aware of your presence everywhere, Lord, and I am overwhelmed with gratitude and praise.

But if from there you seek the LORD your God, you will find him if you seek him with all your heart and with all your soul. Deuteronomy 4:29 (NIV)

I feel God reaching out to me when . . .

AUGUST 24

Prepare me, O Lord, to read your Word in the Scripture this morning. Inspire me by opening my eyes and my heart so I can see the many miracles that You have used to bless my life. May this Bible passage inspire me to be courageous enough to trust You, patient enough to wait on your timing, and humble enough to seek You in everything, through Jesus Christ.

I remain confident of this:
  I will see the goodness of the LORD
  in the land of the living.
Wait for the LORD;
  be strong and take heart
  and wait for the LORD.
Psalm 27:13-14 (NIV)

My favorite Bible passage is . . .

AUGUST 25

Creator God, You have blessed me with vistas of the moon rising flooding me with muted light, and the sun with its fiery fingers greeting me with its glory. My spirit is enlightened as I celebrate the gifts surrounding me in every moment. You are the One who kindles in me the flicker of hope in the midst of darkness. You show me in countless ways that You are here with me—not simply out there beyond me, but by my side when I need your presence. O Lord of wonder, I pause in prayer to remember the gift of your Son, Jesus Christ, my Lord, whose light shines within me, day and night.

You, LORD, keep my lamp burning;
my God turns my darkness into light.
Psalm 18:28 (NIV)

Oregon Coast

AUGUST 26

Blessed Lord, in the power of fresh faith, my soul finds joy; in the light of newly ignited faith, my mind begins to understand; and in the warmth of deepening faith, my heart is recommitted to love boldly. Of all your blessings, O Lord, faith is the first. Let my prayer time lead me to a time of decision:

> show me what is important;
>> take me to where I am most needed;
>>> steer my feet into the pathways of life

so that I might go forth ready to make a difference in this world for You, through your Son, Jesus Christ.

Defend the weak and the fatherless;
  uphold the cause of the poor and the oppressed.
Rescue the weak and the needy;
  deliver them from the hand of the wicked.
Psalm 82:3-4 (NIV)

What is most important to me this day? Would God agree?

AUGUST 27

O God of this new day, how different my life would be if I embraced each sunrise as a greeting from You and every sunset as a benediction flowing from your grace. Help me to abide in You moment by moment so that gratitude becomes my natural response. Whether I'm in the midst of challenges or in the sweetness of celebration, if I can practice the sacrament of the present moment, I can remain grateful in every circumstance.

Hallelujah!

Thank GOD! Pray to him by name!
Tell everyone you meet what he has done!
Sing him songs, belt out hymns,
translate his wonders into music!
Honor his holy name with Hallelujahs,
you who seek GOD. Live a happy life!
Keep your eyes open for GOD, watch for his works;
be alert for signs of his presence.
Psalm 105:1-4 (The Message)

I am so grateful for . . .

AUGUST 28

Ever-present Lord, I turn to You because I face difficult people and prickly situations that I know are beyond my ability to manage. Into your care I lift

children struggling to find a sense of identity;

confusing situations that demand decisions;

loved ones bowed down by anxiety or depression;

relationships strained by too many demands and too little time.

O Lord, You invite me to release my concerns into your watchful, loving care, trusting that You will provide abundantly more than I could ask for or need, and so I lift them to You.

So we're not giving up. How could we! Even though on the outside it often looks like things are falling apart on us, on the inside, where God is making new life, not a day goes by without his unfolding grace. These hard times are small potatoes compared to the coming good times, the lavish celebration prepared for us. There's far more here than meets the eye. The things we see now are here today, gone tomorrow. But the things we can't see now will last forever.

2 Corinthians 4:16-18 (The Message)

Porcupine, Montana

This week I have been pondering and praying over these intriguing words from John Wesley, the founder of the Methodist Church: "Though I am always in haste, I am never in a hurry because I never undertake any more work than I can go through with perfect calmness of spirit."

O Lord of these warm days, with the land vibrant and green, I pause in these moments to be still and worship You. Come near, O Jesus, in this quiet time; come and be my Lord and Companion. Let the peace of your presence bring a hush over my hurriedness. Let the strength of your integrity bring new depth to my character. O Lord, You have granted me the gift of today. Help me to so live in this present moment that I would reflect the joy and peace of a life anchored in You.

Now may the Lord of peace himself give you peace at all times and in every way. The Lord be with all of you. 2 Thessalonians 3:16 (NIV)

I seek God's presence in . . .

Lord of this pilgrimage, I am thankful that You walk with me, calling me to new adventures with You. I know that my fears have robbed me of the courage I need to stand firm. Sometimes preoccupation with myself has clouded my impulse to give freely. At other times, doubting voices have stilled my capacity for risk. Free me from each of these handicaps and lead me to walk boldly with You in faith.

But the Lord is faithful; he will strengthen you and guard you from the evil one. And we are confident in the Lord that you are doing and will continue to do the things we commanded you. May the Lord lead your hearts into a full understanding and expression of the love of God and the patient endurance that comes from Christ. 2 Thessalonians 3:3-5 (NLT)

What fears are dragging me down?

AUGUST 31

Almighty God, the stillness of a mirrored lake invites me to ponder the choices You have placed before me. I have asked for your wise direction, and then an unexpected invitation to travel a different pathway unfolds before me:

You have shown me the wisdom of silence in the face of provocation;

You have opened my eyes to a different way of responding to a loved one;

You have presented a brand new opportunity to grow in my career.

Enable me to see your hand pointing out the way as I seek your will in my life.

I have refused to walk on any evil path,
  so that I may remain obedient to your word.
Psalm 119:101 (NLT)

Grand Teton National Park, Wyoming

SEPTEMBER 1

A few years ago I found an anonymous prayer on a website that I especially liked: "So far today, God, I have done all right. I have not gossiped. I have not lost my temper. I have not been greedy, grumpy, nasty, selfish, or over-indulgent. I am very thankful for that. But in a few moments, God, I'm going to get out of bed. From then on, I'm going to need a lot of help."

O God of faithfulness, wherever I find myself in this adventure called life, I trust that You will meet me there as I open my heart and soul to You. Nudge me into the realization, Lord, that with You a new life, a new vision, and a new joy are always possible.

If you abide in me, and my words abide in you, ask whatever you wish, and it will be done for you. John 15:7 (ESV)

Mackerel Cove, Maine

SEPTEMBER 2

Precious Lord, on this Labor Day weekend, help me to embody your spirit while I am at work. Help me to

offer secret kindnesses with no need for a reward,

extend forgiveness with no hidden agenda,

release anger without any lingering resentment.

As I do so, I glimpse your Kingdom at work in my life and in my world. Lord, guide me as I seek You in the power of your Word. Continue the work You are doing, O Lord, to make me an extraordinary disciple on a mission to serve You in this world, through the power of your Son, Jesus Christ.

Jesus also used this illustration: "The Kingdom of Heaven is like the yeast a woman used in making bread. Even though she put only a little yeast in three measures of flour, it permeated every part of the dough. Matthew 13:33 (NLT)

Today I can offer kindness to . . .

SEPTEMBER 3

Lord of my life, I turn to You trusting that never once have You left me to fend for myself. You have promised to walk with me always. Hear me as I lift in prayer those who find themselves in lonely places where the shadows darken the path, and those who are engulfed in tunnels that seem to be impenetrable to even a glimmer of light. I pray for others bound by life circumstances that are breaking their spirits. In each situation that is beyond my control, I turn to You, praying that by the touch of your hand, each one might be set free. It is my deepest prayer that your peace would enfold this world, touching it with a glimpse of your Kingdom, as I pray in the name of your Son, Jesus Christ.

Can a mother forget the baby at her breast
*   and have no compassion on the child she has borne?*
Though she may forget,
*   I will not forget you!*
See, I have engraved you on the palms of my hands;
*   your walls are ever before me.*
Isaiah 49:15-16 (NIV)

I release these situations to God . . .

Acadia National Park, Maine

SEPTEMBER 4

God of all glory, your magnificence shines through this entire world. All of nature beckons me to enjoy You on this Sabbath day of rest. The lofty pines serve as sentinels declaring your praise, calling me to worship. The sun, ready to peek over the distant horizon, invites me into the celebration of a brand new day. You created the Sabbath, O Lord, that I might know that You are God, and I am not. O Lord of wonder, I pause for this prayer time to remember who You are and that your grace reaches out to me just as You have reached out to countless others in ages past.

So you'll go out in joy,
   you'll be led into a whole and complete life.
The mountains and hills will lead the parade,
   bursting with song.
All the trees of the forest will join the procession,
   exuberant with applause.
No more thistles, but giant sequoias,
   no more thornbushes, but stately pines—
Monuments to me, to GOD,
   living and lasting evidence of GOD.
Isaiah 55:12-13 (The Message)

SEPTEMBER 5

Caring and sensitive God, as I rest in your holy presence, I come with an open and willing heart, ready to allow You to see the whole of my being—all my hopes, my dreams, my joys, and my plans. I also bring my failures, my struggles, my disappointments, and my pain to You. I have discovered that when I surrender everything and trust You, You begin the work of making me whole and prepare me again to live the life You have always envisioned for me.

The LORD is merciful and gracious,
*   slow to anger and abounding in steadfast love.*
He will not always accuse,
*   nor will he keep his anger forever.*
He does not deal with us according to our sins,
*   nor repay us according to our iniquities.*
For as the heavens are high above the earth,
*   so great is his steadfast love toward those who fear him;*
as far as the east is from the west,
*   so far he removes our transgressions from us.*
Psalm 103:8-12 (NRSV)

I trust You to . . .

SEPTEMBER 6

O Lord, You are my place of shelter, my refuge from the tempest and storm of life. When the world seems to close in around me, help me to remember Jesus' response to the stresses of this life. Lead me to a quiet place of prayer, for when I have been pushed beyond my limits, it is only there that I can find your peace. It is there that I can simply offer the emptiness of my own heart. It is there that You fill the void with waves of peace cascading into my soul.

You are my hiding place;
  you will protect me from trouble
  and surround me with songs of deliverance.
Psalm 32:7 (NIV)

What are the frightened places in my heart that need God's comfort?

SEPTEMBER 7

O Wondrous God, whose creativity knows no limits, I celebrate the beauty of this universe that swirls around me in endless complexity, the teeming, vibrant, sparkling, energizing life that You have spoken into being. And I am grateful that each person who has been formed in your image has the unmistakable print of originality within. You have made me to be creative, bringing my own unique gifts to this world. You have entrusted me with the means to plant the seeds of your Kingdom here on earth through offering my solace to someone who needs a gentle word; extending myself just a little bit further than where I feel comfortable; dreaming and sharing a vision for what could yet be accomplished in your name.

Thank you, O God, for helping me understand my purpose in your universe.

Many are the plans in a person's heart,
*   but it is the LORD's purpose that prevails.*
Proverbs 19:21 (NIV)

Danby, Vermont

SEPTEMBER 8

Eternal God, perhaps no one on earth knows about the burdens I am carrying, but You know. So, I want to be open to all the ways You communicate with me. Yet, with my incessant hurrying, my mindless pursuit of entertainment, and my discomfort with silence, so often I put up roadblocks to sensing your guidance. Hour by hour help me to intentionally open my spirit to You. Breathe fresh life into my listening, my speaking, and my praying so that each one might be a means of experiencing your presence in the midst of my life.

Desperate, I throw myself on you:
  you are my God!
Hour by hour I place my days in your hand,
  safe from the hands out to get me.
Warm me, your servant, with a smile;
  save me because you love me.
Psalm 31:14-16 (The Message)

What are my roadblocks to a deepening discipleship?

SEPTEMBER 9

God of tenderness, I know that I live my ordinary life and that your Spirit lives in me. Yet, sometimes I carry burdens that are heavier than I can manage on my own. Lord, when I become discouraged, help me to sense, even in the midst of problems and pain, a glimpse of your glory, a window into your world. I yearn for your Holy Spirit to embrace, energize, and re-create me. Then take my wounded spirit and empower me to live and serve You anew as your hands and heart in my world.

Let your servants see what you're best at—
   the ways you rule and bless your children.
And let the loveliness of our Lord, our God, rest on us,
   confirming the work that we do.
   Oh, yes. Affirm the work that we do!
Psalm 90:16-17 (The Message)

I am energized to . . .

SEPTEMBER 10

Majestic God, thank you for all of creation's riches—the freshness of the wind, the bounty of the fall harvest, and the sun that brings all the shapes and splashes of color to light.

I remember the gifts of this week—a listening ear, a gentle touch, an understanding smile. Thank you for the deep sense of peace that arises within me when I surrender to You and look forward to a quiet metamorphosis through your Holy Spirit in the days ahead.

Yes, I am the vine; you are the branches. Those who remain in me, and I in them, will produce much fruit. For apart from me you can do nothing. John 15:5 (NLT)

Napa Valley, California

SEPTEMBER 11

Precious Lord, in the midst of my community of faith so many challenges arise. My mind's eye captures the faces of the ones I know who need your presence today. Abba Father, I trust that when my words fail me in prayer, You hear the deepest cries of my heart. You travel to the ends of the earth to embrace each wandering one; You will watch for hours by the bedside of one who is ill; You stand strong with the ones who know weakness or failing. I am amazed that You see beauty in each one of us, that You can see the promise of a life surrendered and then transformed by your grace. O Lord, may each person know a moment of living with purpose and enthusiasm and courage, and may these moments multiply through Jesus Christ who promises abundant life.

For if you remain silent at this time, relief and deliverance for the Jews will arise from another place, but you and your father's family will perish. And who knows but that you have come to your royal position for such a time as this? Esther 4:14 (NIV)

I pray for the courage to . . .

SEPTEMBER 12

O God, whose grace encircles my life, thank you for the promise of fresh beginnings, as your light illuminates my world with each new sunrise. Thank you for every touch of healing peace and strengthening hope that You have given me this week. My heart overflows with gratitude as I recognize your invitation to come into your presence, bringing all that I am, all my dreams and my hopes, all my faith and all my doubts. I know that You, the Lord of the universe, care enough to hear the whispered longings of my heart.

The fear of the LORD is the beginning of wisdom,
    and the knowledge of the Holy One is insight.
Proverbs 9:10 (ESV)

I am hungry for . . .

SEPTEMBER 13

Almighty God, I enter your presence with contented joy, for You are the One who loves me beyond all measure. The daily reminder of your goodness is reflected all around me in the bounty that dazzles my senses. Thank you, O Lord, for the rhythm of the changing seasons, the snowy egrets prancing across my lawn, the gleam of fireflies in the moonlight, and the infinite stars of the galaxies beyond. In these moments I stop to recognize that You alone are God, the source of all goodness, and You are worthy of all praise. May my worship on this one day grant meaning to all the rest of the days of the week.

The choir and trumpets made one voice of praise and thanks to GOD—orchestra and choir in perfect harmony singing and playing praise to GOD:
> *Yes! God is good!*
> *His loyal love goes on forever!*
2 Chronicles 5:13a (The Message)

Maple, Danby, Vermont

SEPTEMBER 14

O God of goodness, in the silence of prayer, I enter your presence with honesty and openness, trusting You to redirect my ways. I know far too well the struggles and limitations I bring with me this day. Yet, I come to You trusting that your mercy reaches out to me even in the midst of my failures. Pick me up and remind me that your love and forgiveness always embrace me, especially in the darkest experiences of my life.

And in my brighter moments, I remember that You have created me with talents to be used in service. You have gifted me to bless others. Let this be my intent and prayer today.

You are the light of the world. A town built on a hill cannot be hidden. Neither do people light a lamp and put it under a bowl. Instead they put it on its stand, and it gives light to everyone in the house. In the same way, let your light shine before others, that they may see your good deeds and glorify your Father in heaven. Matthew 5:14-16 (NIV)

I open myself to God's direction as I use my gifts to . . .

SEPTEMBER 15

Every week when we pray the Lord's Prayer, we say "Thy will be done." To me, these four words mean surrender—of my life, of all my situations—to God. But, I often struggle to know when I have really surrendered a situation into God's hands. When I mentioned this doubt to a friend, she said, "I know that I have completely surrendered something to God when I am not attached to the outcome."

Gracious God, I am slowly discovering the paradox of experiencing all of life with You. The pain and struggles I have known as a part of being alive are the very road leading me to You. I am learning that honest surrender brings boundless freedom, that vulnerability is really courage, and that stepping into the wide unknown is the beginning of an adventure with You. Lord, help me to remember that I don't have to dictate what will happen because I am learning to lean on You, instead trusting that You will open my eyes to the next right step.

Love the LORD your God with all your heart and with all your soul and with all your strength. These commandments that I give you today are to be on your hearts. Impress them on your children. Talk about them when you sit at home and when you walk along the road, when you lie down and when you get up. Deuteronomy 6:5-7 (NIV)

Today my next step of surrender is . . .

SEPTEMBER 16

Lord of abundant life, who created a world filled with infinite variety, today I am re-awakened to the awe of being alive. Encircled by creation's gifts of rivers and ponds, woods and wildflowers, marshes and meadows, I pause to breathe deeply and take it all in, celebrating that You are the source of it all. As I reflect on your goodness, I yearn to grow closer to You. Show me the way, Lord. Show me the way.

O LORD, I give my life to you.
  I trust in you, my God!
Psalm 25:1-2a (NLT)

Kittery, Maine

SEPTEMBER 17

Lord, my God, who never turns away when any child of yours calls out in prayer, I reach out today to take your outstretched hand. I call out to You to hear my prayer, for I am your child and like a child, I often lose my way. When I face myself, I know I am not who I want to be for You. I know my impatience, my selfishness, my resentments, and my anger. Forgive me, O Lord, and help me to accept your forgiveness and move on, with my sins behind me and your hope before me.

The one who looks at me is seeing the one who sent me. I have come into the world as a light, so that no one who believes in me should stay in darkness. "If anyone hears my words but does not keep them, I do not judge that person. For I did not come to judge the world, but to save it." John 12:45-47 (NIV)

I need to make amends to . . .

SEPTEMBER 18

O God of the Sabbath rest, on this morning when my inner world is quieted, I pause to reflect on the moments of genuine joy in this past week:

a genuine connection with a good friend,

a meaningful conversation,

a moment of awe-filled wonder,

a breakthrough in a challenging situation,

and I give You thanks. O Lord of this new day, walk with me through all the events I have planned. But even more, I ask that You would open my heart in surrender, trusting You to fill each of the spaces on my calendar with what You are inviting me to do and to experience.

Shout for joy to the LORD, all the earth.
Worship the LORD with gladness;
come before him with joyful songs.
Know that the LORD is God.
It is he who made us, and we are his;
we are his people, the sheep of his pasture.
Enter his gates with thanksgiving
and his courts with praise;
give thanks to him and praise his name.
For the LORD is good and his love endures forever;
his faithfulness continues through all generations.
Psalm 100 (NIV)

My joys include . . .

SEPTEMBER 19

Lord of all creation, from the dawn of time, You have sculpted the mountain ranges; You have carved out the craggy caverns; You have splashed the landscapes with colors. You have filled my senses with the sights and sounds of nature teeming with life—from the scampering of squirrels to the sparkle of a distant lake. Every bit of it proclaims your majesty, and when I pause to drink in your bounty with a grateful heart, I am renewed and refreshed.

Out of the north he comes in golden splendor;
God comes in awesome majesty.
The Almighty is beyond our reach and exalted in power;
in his justice and great righteousness, he does not oppress.
Therefore, people revere him,
for does he not have regard for all the wise in heart?
Job 37:22-24 (NIV)

Denali National Park, Alaska

SEPTEMBER 20

Lord of the quiet whisper, as I begin my day, You remind me once again that You come to me in quiet interludes of simplicity and silence. This morning I seek You, asking You to refocus my thoughts on your presence. I remember that You greet me in every ordinary moment, as I pause to begin my day with a steaming mug of coffee or as I take a moment to greet a stranger with a kind word. In each moment I pause to be mindful of your presence right in the midst of my life.

(Jesus said to his disciples) *"But when you pray, go into your room, close the door and pray to your Father, who is unseen. Then your Father, who sees what is done in secret, will reward you. And when you pray, do not keep on babbling like pagans, for they think they will be heard because of their many words. Do not be like them, for your Father knows what you need before you ask him.*
"This, then, is how you should pray:

> *"Our Father in heaven,*
> *hallowed be your name,*
> *your kingdom come,*
> *your will be done, on earth as it is in heaven.*
> *Give us today our daily bread.*
> *And forgive us our debts,*
> *as we also have forgiven our debtors.*
> *And lead us not into temptation,*
> *but deliver us from the evil one."*

Matthew 6:6-13 (NIV)

I am mindful of your presence when . . .

SEPTEMBER 21

Blessed Lord, I pray with faith and hope because You have already blessed my life so richly. You have again provided exactly what I need. I trust that your love for me is real and reaches to the ends of the earth. As your Word proclaims, I can go nowhere that You are not already there, waiting for me, ready to meet me and to lead me back home. Thank you for those who have cared enough to speak the truth in love to me—even when I find myself busy criticizing them. Thank you for the precious insights that have come after struggles, for wisdom and maturity that often emerge the hard way, and for all the grace-filled second chances You have given me. Thank you for those who walk alongside me, showing me that You don't just call extraordinary people to follow Jesus: You call ordinary people and make them extraordinary by your grace.

(Jesus said) *"Why do you look at the speck of sawdust in your brother's eye and pay no attention to the plank in your own eye? How can you say to your brother, 'Let me take the speck out of your eye,' when all the time there is a plank in your own eye? You hypocrite, first take the plank out of your own eye, and then you will see clearly to remove the speck from your brother's eye.* Matthew 7:3-5 (NIV)

Who are the special people who provide me with grace and truth?

SEPTEMBER 22

At the end of a women's Bible study, one of the participants said, "I used to pray, 'Lord be with me' until I realized God is always with me. I changed my prayer to: 'God, help me to be with You.'" That is God's invitation to me every moment as I seek His presence in prayer.

God of the open sea and zephyr winds, God of the endless coastline and untracked forests, God of the yearning heart and questing mind, God of the cloud by day and pillar of fire by night, You are the One who is always before me, opening my eyes to the wonders all around that underscore your glory. So once again I am in awe before You, humbled that You call me your own.

Because of your great compassion you did not abandon them in the wilderness. By day the pillar of cloud did not fail to guide them on their path, nor the pillar of fire by night to shine on the way they were to take. Nehemiah 9:19 (NIV)

Crocus Bay, Anguilla

Laurie Bohlke

SEPTEMBER 23

Loving God, in all of my relationships, help me to think before I speak, pause before I offer an unsolicited opinion, close my mouth before I am tempted to gossip or betray a confidence, and breathe deeply before I react in anger. I ask for your forgiveness for the missteps I have taken. I need your cleansing love to help me release my shame so that I might believe that I am both forgiven and freed.

Listen, open your ears, harness your desire to speak, and don't get worked up into a rage so easily, my brothers and sisters. Human anger *is a futile exercise that* will never produce God's kind of justice *in this world.*
James 1:19-20 (The Voice)

I need healing in my relationship with . . .

SEPTEMBER 24

Blessed Lord, grant me the gift of faith, trusting that no matter my circumstances, I matter to You. Grant me the hope that blesses each moment—that in spite of the doubt or hurt or fear, You are always there with me. Grant me the love that has the vision beyond any present situation to see your face in the ones around me. I offer this prayer and all the deepest prayers of my heart in the power of Jesus Christ.

Instead, we will speak the truth in love, growing in every way more and more like Christ, who is the head of his body, the church. He makes the whole body fit together perfectly. As each part does its own special work, it helps the other parts grow, so that the whole body is healthy and growing and full of love. Ephesians 4:15-16 (NLT)

I entrust to You . . .

SEPTEMBER 25

Omnipotent God, whose signature I see in the creation of the universe, help me to look for your handwriting in this quiet moment, among these people. As I worship, I ask that You would gather up my temporary praise and unite it to your timeless rhythms, your ageless melodies, and your everlasting joyful noise that permeates all of creation. Breathe your life into my singing, my praying, my speaking, my listening, and my touching, so that each might become a means to both praise You and experience your presence. In worship I reach out to You, O God, knowing that You have already enfolded me in your arms.

Hallelujah!
I give thanks to GOD with everything I've got—
Wherever good people gather, and in the congregation.
Psalm 111:1 (The Message)

Damariscotta, Maine

SEPTEMBER 26

I have discovered in recent years that while pain in life is inevitable, suffering is really optional.

Most Holy One, when I am confused by the complexities of my life, guide me so I can stop seeking to make sense of everything and instead start trusting that your hand is at work in all things. When I find myself vulnerable and unable to control my usually well-ordered world, enable me to experience the freedom of letting go and allowing You to be at work in my situation, bringing wholeness and resolution. O Lord, even when I am immersed in a storm of suffering, help me to walk in trust as You reveal my path one step at a time.

Jesus said to the people who believed in him, "You are truly my disciples if you remain faithful to my teachings. And you will know the truth, and the truth will set you free." John 8:31-32 (NLT)

I need to let go of . . .

SEPTEMBER 27

Gentle Teacher, You remind me often that discipleship is more than worrying about my own life; it is reaching out to others with the grace You have offered to me. Help me to care about each one of your children. Grant me the willingness to reach out to love the ones who are difficult for me to love. I pray for the ones whose hearts are pounding with stress; the ones who want to let go of a problem but cannot release it into your care; the ones who have created a wall of protection against hurt; the ones who battle daily to forgive one near to them; and the ones who carry a quiet grief alone.

Let my prayer be for my heart to know generosity of spirit so that I can look beyond my own needs to have the time, space, and resources to offer your grace to others in daily quiet acts of service and mercy.

Your beauty should not come from outward adornment, such as elaborate hairstyles and the wearing of gold jewelry or fine clothes. Rather, it should be that of your inner self, the unfading beauty of a gentle and quiet spirit, which is of great worth in God's sight. 1 Peter 3:3-4 (NIV)

Empower me to . . .

SEPTEMBER 28

O Lord of all, I am grateful for those moments when I experience the inconceivable surprise of living—those eternal moments of grace-filled awe that always lead me back to You. The glory of life shouts out in the effortless flight of birds soaring on the wings of morning, the gentle caress of the warm breeze, and the exquisite intricacy with which You created each person. Grant me a wide-angled lens to see the panorama of life through your eyes.

The whole earth is filled with awe at your wonders;
*   where morning dawns, where evening fades,*
*   you call forth songs of joy.*
Psalm 65:8 (NIV)

Snow geese, Vermont

SEPTEMBER 29

O Lord of peace, You beckon me to join You in a daily time of solitude, but I come to this time of prayer with my own loud distractions. I am so often blinded by the incessant demands that claim my days—phone calls to be returned, projects placed in my hands, people's needs that cry out for my attention. And in the midst of it all, I often feel as if my life is out of balance, with little energy left for the important and meaningful in my life. Lord, whatever mood I may be in right now, I have the same desire—to know your distinctive presence in the midst of all that clutters my life. I long to sense the comfort of your grace centering my spirit once again. Then I can breathe a deep sigh and know I am back at home in your presence.

Now may our Lord Jesus Christ himself and God our Father, who loved us and by his grace gave us eternal comfort and a wonderful hope, comfort you and strengthen you in every good thing you do and say.
2 Thessalonians 2:16-17 (NLT)

Today I do not need to be ruled by clutter. I can choose to . . .

SEPTEMBER 30

We had so much rain last week that by Wednesday, I was really grumpy. The funny thing was that once I opened the "grumpy closet," everything flew out. Pretty soon, I was all over grumpy. Then that night I went to a church meeting, and someone talked about her gratitude for the rain, because her flowers were so much more beautiful. So I opened the gratitude closet, and a funny thing happened. Everything shifted.

Thank you, Lord, for the people You send into my life to remind me of the power of joy-filled thinking. Help me to remain open for your messages, so that I can find the door to the gratitude closet, no matter how grumpy I feel.

(The Apostle Paul wrote) *I always thank my God when I pray for you, Philemon, because I keep hearing about your faith in the Lord Jesus and your love for all of God's people. And I am praying that you will put into action the generosity that comes from your faith as you understand and experience all the good things we have in Christ. Your love has given me much joy and comfort, my brother, for your kindness has often refreshed the hearts of God's people.* Philemon 1:4-7 (NLT)

My gratitude closet contains . . .

Danby, Vermont

OCTOBER 1

Judaism uses an ancient Passover song, a kind of litany to which the response is always *Dayenu*! (It would have been enough.) The prayer lists all the wonderful works of God one-by-one, and after each one the congregation proclaims *Dayenu*—as if to say, how much is it going to take for us to know that God is with us? Instead of breeding discontentment, this kind of prayer is building gratitude.

Gracious God, at harvest time, your majesty seems to burst the bounds of creation. Your glory is ever-present in the canopy of brilliant blue in the skies above, and the lush green and earthy brown of the land below. You have given me one more day simply to be alive—to savor your gifts: my beating heart, the safety net of family and friends, precious freedom, education, abundant clean water, more than enough food, a roof over my head, and your eternal love. And in these moments, Yahweh, You give me the spiritual eyes to see your fingerprints all around me. And I take a moment to whisper, "*Dayenu*. It would have been enough."

Philip said, "Lord, show us the Father and that will be enough for us."
John 14:8 (NIV)

OCTOBER 2

Spirit of the Living God, I am grateful for your whispers of grace, love and hope—and for the gift of forgiveness. They are the realities that keep me trusting your goodness in all of life. As I rest in You this day, let your love so blaze that my life might spark hope, inspiration, and peace in the people I meet in your name.

Now when He was asked by the Pharisees when the kingdom of God would come, He answered them and said, "The kingdom of God does not come with observation; nor will they say, 'See here!' or 'See there!' For indeed, the kingdom of God is within you." Luke 17:20-21 (NKJV)

Today I can offer kindness and respect to . . .

OCTOBER 3

O God of new beginnings, You place within my heart the desire for relationship and the hope for community. Yet I have drifted away from meaningful friendships, and I have been in conflict with ones I love. I have even been estranged from family and friends. I turn to You knowing that it is often difficult to move from the comfort of what I know to risk the discomfort of the unknown. Lord, give me the wisdom to know when I need to reach out, when to make the first move, and when to take one step closer to reconciliation so that I can honor You within your community of believers.

Since this is the kind of life we have chosen, the life of the Spirit, let us make sure that we do not just hold it as an idea in our heads or a sentiment in our hearts, but work out its implications in every detail of our lives. That means we will not compare ourselves with each other as if one of us were better and another worse. We have far more interesting things to do with our lives. Each of us is an original. Galatians 5:25-26 (The Message)

Lord, help me to risk reaching out to . . .

OCTOBER 4

This week I remembered a quotation from the second century theologian, Irenaeus: "The glory of God is man (woman) fully alive." The question I have been pondering is, "What would it take to be fully alive?"

O God of wonder, on this morning I am filled with the joy of being alive. The gauzy mists of morning have gently invited me into this day. As I anticipate the plans before me, I ponder all the ways You have been at work in my life, the moments of laughter blasting through the yoke of weariness and the joyful explosion of melody that stirs my spirit. I know that You have brought me to this prayer time to prepare my heart for the message of your love poured out in Jesus Christ. So, dear Lord, hear my prayers, and, in the silence that follows, I will listen for your response.

When Jesus spoke again to the people, he said, "I am the light of the world. Whoever follows me will never walk in darkness, but will have the light of life." John 8:12 (NIV)

Oregon coast

OCTOBER 5

Oh God of goodness, in the quiet of this moment, I enter your presence with honesty and openness, trusting You to re-orient my ways. Despite the struggles and limitations I bring with me today, I come to You knowing that your mercy shelters me under the protection of your wings. Even in the midst of my failures, You pick me up and remind me that your grace is more than enough. Hear me as I open my innermost thoughts to You.

Often at night I lie in bed and remember You,
  meditating on Your *greatness* till morning *smiles through my window*.
You have been my *constant* helper;
  therefore, I sing for joy under the protection of Your wings.
My soul clings to You;
  Your right hand *reaches down and* holds me up.
Psalm 63:6-8 (The Voice)

Where do I need God to re-orient me today?

O Spring of joyful life, my thirsting spirit comes to You to drink deeply of your living water. Sometimes I come celebrating with lighthearted laughter, but today my spirit is bogged down, and I have limited my capacity for joy. So I come to You, believing that You are the source of renewing hope. As I find myself re-evaluating my life, keep me from defining myself by the categories of my past as the blueprint for my future. Free me from ruminating remorse, nagging guilt, or clinging fears. Usher me into the sunshine of your grace as I invite the winds of your Holy Spirit to sweep me in new directions.

You're my cave to hide in,
my cliff to climb.
Be my safe leader,
be my true mountain guide.
Free me from hidden traps;
I want to hide in you.
I've put my life in your hands.
You won't drop me,
you'll never let me down.
Psalm 31:3-5 (The Message)

The wisdom of your Holy Spirit is guiding me to . . .

OCTOBER 7

Compassionate God, the prayers I offer are a tapestry of my love and concern for the people You have placed in my life. I pray for those who need healing of body, mind, or spirit and for each one who cares for them. I pray for those who are being tossed and shaken by the storms of life. I pray for those who are confused and discouraged by situations that are beyond their control. And now I pause for a moment to take a deep breath and offer You all the other concerns of my heart. Hear my prayers, Lord.

You are my shelter, O Eternal One—*my soul's sanctuary!*
    Shield me from shame;
    rescue me by Your righteousness
Hear me, Lord! Turn Your ear in my direction.
    Come quick! Save me!
Be my rock, my shelter,
    my fortress of salvation!
Psalm 31:1-2 (The Voice)

Minturn, Colorado

OCTOBER 8

Life-changing Lord, give me the eyes to glimpse You today in the people and situations I encounter, for each one can invite me to experience You anew. Though You may sometimes hide yourself in the ones I least expect, may I still recognize You and say, "Lord, here I am; let me serve You." Dear Lord, help me live this day reflectively and attentively, ready for You to break into my world, surprising me and others by your grace.

(The Apostle Paul wrote) *What I'm getting at, friends, is that you should simply keep on doing what you've done from the beginning. When I was living among you, you lived in responsive obedience. Now that I'm separated from you, keep it up. Better yet, redouble your efforts. Be energetic in your life of salvation, reverent and sensitive before God. That energy is God's energy, an energy deep within you, God himself willing and working at what will give him the most pleasure.* Philippians 2:12-13 (The Message)

Today I can serve You by . . .

OCTOBER 9

Dear God, as I prepare for worship, I look forward to the beauty of music that sweeps over my soul, and to your Word leaping into life through Scripture and sermon. Grant me an open and willing spirit to hear your message for me this morning. And I pray that in these twenty-four hours You have given to me, I might know the deep joy of following in the path of Jesus by making life a little better for the people I encounter.

For we are God's handiwork, created in Christ Jesus to do good works, which God prepared in advance for us to do. Ephesians 2:10 (NIV)

God's message to me today is . . .

OCTOBER 10

Gentle Teacher, thank you for the wisdom of the years that helps me to look back with eyes of grace and acceptance, remembering the truly important parts of life. Then, help me to turn from the past as You teach me to seek You and to be fully present in each moment of my day. I invite You to transform my shortcomings into a testimony of what You can accomplish in a life surrendered to You. Increase my sensitivity to the people around me so that your love might shine through me in the name of Jesus.

Stand up in the presence of the aged, show respect for the elderly and revere your God. I am the LORD. Leviticus 19: 32 (NIV)

Santorini, Greece

OCTOBER 11

Almighty God, each day You surround me like a steady breeze. You give me the gift of fresh possibility through your life-giving renewal as I abide in You. Help me to walk so closely to Jesus that my steps will be steady, my hope firm, and my trust secure.

Then, grant me a humble spirit, O Lord, so that I might be one who serves. Fill me so that I might give out of my abundance. Guide me so that I might venture with courage on the journey You have entrusted to me, with Jesus, my Savior.

For even the Son of Man came not to be served but to serve others and to give his life as a ransom for many. Mark 10:45 (NLT)

A fresh possibility that awaits me is . . .

God of healing, no one on earth knows about the struggles and burdens that I am carrying, but You know. You invite me to bring everything to You in prayer: friends who are enduring serious physical problems; those who are facing uphill challenges in parenting; others who are bearing the burden of care-giving that sometimes feels like a privilege and at other times feels life-draining; some who are facing financial difficulties and need a sense of direction this very week.

Each one needs your healing touch. Lord, I have hurts and hopes, discouragements and dreams. I pray for your touch to encourage me and uplift me. So, I am reaching out to You, trusting that You are already reaching out to me.

Listen to my prayer, O God.
   Do not ignore my cry for help!
Please listen and answer me,
   for I am overwhelmed by my troubles.
Psalm 55:1-2 (NLT)

I need God's grace today in facing moments . . .

OCTOBER 13

Loving Lord, thank you for settling me in a community, for my family who nurtures my growth, for friends who love me by choice, for companions at work who share my burdens, for strangers who welcome me in their midst, for children who lighten my moments with delight. But most of all, I stand amazed that your love reaches out to each of us in Jesus Christ, my Savior. So thank you for your grace and for one more experience of your presence; thank you for my life and one more day to share your love.

Jesus replied: "'Love the Lord your God with all your heart and with all your soul and with all your mind.' This is the first and greatest commandment. And the second is like it: 'Love your neighbor as yourself.' All the Law and the Prophets hang on these two commandments." Matthew 22:37-40 (NIV)

Acadia National Park, Maine

OCTOBER 16

Eternal God, make me vulnerable enough so that I might speak with calm humility. Make me mindful of others so that I might care deeply. Make me one of a community of bridge builders so that I might glimpse a little of your Kingdom here on earth. And in the midst of the world's turbulence, help me make space in my heart for the hearing of your almost imperceptible whisper, for I want to know You and serve You in the name and by the power of Jesus Christ, my Lord.

(Jesus said) *"Again, I tell you that if two of you on earth agree about anything they ask for, it will be done for them by my Father in heaven. For where two or three come together in my name, there am I with them."*
Matthew 18:19-20 (NIV)

Acadia National Park, Maine

OCTOBER 15

O Lord of all life, as I rest in You, I lift up whatever troubles my mind today. Soften my heart so that I might release my most difficult relationships into your care, neither trying to control the outcome nor hardening myself to your guiding hand in them. When I feel so overwhelmed by life that I cannot even imagine that You care, plant the seed of hope that life could be different with your steady presence.

In my ordinary days, I know your Spirit lives in me. Through your grace alone, when I become discouraged, your Holy Spirit embraces and energizes me. You take my wounded spirit and empower me to love and serve You anew as I become your hands and heart in my world. I pray in the name of Jesus, who showed me a life built upon seeking and doing your will.

All that passing laws against sin did was produce more lawbreakers. But sin didn't, and doesn't, have a chance in competition with the aggressive forgiveness we call grace. When it's sin versus grace, grace wins hands down. All sin can do is threaten us with death, and that's the end of it. Grace, because God is putting everything together again through the Messiah, invites us into life—a life that goes on and on and on, world without end. Romans 5:20-21 (The Message)

Today your seeds of hope lead me to . . .

OCTOBER 16

Eternal God, make me vulnerable enough so that I might speak with calm humility. Make me mindful of others so that I might care deeply. Make me one of a community of bridge builders so that I might glimpse a little of your Kingdom here on earth. And in the midst of the world's turbulence, help me make space in my heart for the hearing of your almost imperceptible whisper, for I want to know You and serve You in the name and by the power of Jesus Christ, my Lord.

(Jesus said) *"Again, I tell you that if two of you on earth agree about anything they ask for, it will be done for them by my Father in heaven. For where two or three come together in my name, there am I with them."*
Matthew 18:19-20 (NIV)

Acadia National Park, Maine

Loving Lord, thank you for settling me in a community, for my family who nurtures my growth, for friends who love me by choice, for companions at work who share my burdens, for strangers who welcome me in their midst, for children who lighten my moments with delight. But most of all, I stand amazed that your love reaches out to each of us in Jesus Christ, my Savior. So thank you for your grace and for one more experience of your presence; thank you for my life and one more day to share your love.

Jesus replied: "'Love the Lord your God with all your heart and with all your soul and with all your mind.' This is the first and greatest commandment. And the second is like it: 'Love your neighbor as yourself.' All the Law and the Prophets hang on these two commandments." Matthew 22:37-40 (NIV)

Acadia National Park, Maine

The Scriptures describe two kinds of time: *Kairos* and *Chronos*. *Chronos* is time that can be measured by a clock in seconds, minutes, hours, and days. *Kairos* time is altogether different. It represents the moments God breaks through *Chronos* to gift us with the Holy Spirit in one eternal moment.

God near at hand, wherever I find myself, I trust that You will meet me as I open my heart and soul to You. I worship You, for I know that You are the center of my existence. Lead me to pay attention to all those coincidences, which are really *Kairos* moments, your unique messages to me. Nudge me in the realization, Lord, that with You a new life, a new vision, and a new joy are forever possible.

And I will be your Father,
  and you will be my sons and daughters,
  says the LORD Almighty.
2 Corinthians 6:18 (NLT)

I remember a *Kairos* moment recently . . .

OCTOBER 17

Merciful God, in prayer I gather up my concerns—my own stumbling blocks, my worries over loved ones, my burdens over this world and its challenges. Help me to discern that which I am powerless to change and also give to me the boldness to risk changing what I can change in my own situation and in my world. Help me to release my fears by taking one step of faith through the fear. And then deliver me from the temptation to snatch back what I have entrusted to You.

. . . Don't be afraid, I've redeemed you.
I've called your name. You're mine.
When you're in over your head, I'll be there with you.
When you're in rough waters, you will not go down.
When you're between a rock and a hard place,
it won't be a dead end—
Because I am GOD, your personal God,
The Holy of Israel, your Savior . . .
Isaiah 43:1b-3a (The Message)

I want to be bold enough to try . . .

Lord, my Counselor, I come as I am into your presence without deceit or pretension, inviting You to search my heart. Yet, sometimes I am afraid of the silence, wondering if your grace includes me. O Lord, touch me when I need a tangible reassurance of your love through a word or a God moment this morning. Help me to experience a renewed sense of your purpose for my life. And then, rooted in your acceptance, enable me to live a life reflecting the glory of your presence within me, so that I might offer an open, accepting space for others in your name.

(Jesus said) *I will show you what it's like when someone comes to me, listens to my teaching, and then follows it. It is like a person building a house who digs deep and lays the foundation on solid rock. When the floodwaters rise and break against that house, it stands firm because it is well built.*
Luke 6:47-48 (NLT)

To connect with God I could . . .

OCTOBER 19

Lord of eternity, all of creation declares your praise this morning. I ponder the reflection of autumn colors in a pond's stillness, a deer leaping across an open meadow, and a long, lazy river inviting me to kick off my shoes and rest a while. Thank you for granting me the gift of this solitary place.

Thank you for friends who call forth the best in me and gently love me, even when I am difficult to love. Lord, You instill unique gifts in each person, so help me understand and develop mine so that my life can display your glory as brilliantly as this fall morning.

There are different kinds of spiritual gifts, but the same Spirit is the source of them all. There are different kinds of service, but we serve the same Lord.
1 Corinthians 12:4-5 (NLT)

Emerald Lake, Vermont

O God of infinite patience, as I reflect on this week past, I come before You, aware of the missteps I have taken. In order to start fresh, I need to ask You to wipe my slate clean. I know that when I am faced with stress-filled circumstances, my default reactions can often be troublesome—to myself and to others. I have found myself irritable, angry, and sometimes, callously indifferent. Father, I ask that You would forgive my thoughtlessness, my hurtful ways, and my inability to even whisper the words, "I'm sorry; please forgive me," to the ones I love. O Lord, help me to remember that while You freely offer me the gift of forgiveness, it was very costly for You because it came from Jesus' life poured out in love for others. And then savoring that awareness, help me to remember to offer the same forgiveness that I have received from You.

Finally, I confessed all my sins to you
*   and stopped trying to hide my guilt.*
I said to myself, "I will confess my rebellion to the LORD."
*   And you forgave me! All my guilt is gone.*
Psalm 32:5 (NLT)

I am aware that I need forgiveness for . . .

OCTOBER 21

God of the wounded heart, as much as I hate to admit it, sometimes I need the storms of life. I need the thunderbolts jarring me enough to awaken me from my hopelessness and complacency. I need lightning flashes bright enough to bring clarity to my jumbled confusion. I need the crashing waves to remind me that as much as I would like to control all of life, ultimately my security lies in trusting You. Take the struggles I bring to You as I surrender those people and situations that fuel my anxious worries. You minister to all of my tired hopes and my worn dreams. O Lord, lift the deep fatigue from my spirit and replace it with your abiding joy.

My soul weeps, and trouble weighs me down;
  give me strength *so I can stand* according to Your word.
Psalm 119:28 (The Voice)

I trust God to be at work in . . .

God of the Covenant, I am grateful for everything that makes this day a gift from your outstretched hand. Your faithfulness stretches across the heavens, and your love spans the farthest reaches of the stars. Still, You reach out to each one who calls out to You, seeking your presence and strength. Gracious God, as I enter these Sabbath moments, teach me how to pause for mini retreats—to slow down enough to hear the soothing lullaby of birds at twilight or the gentle whisper of leaves rustling in the wind. You reveal yourself when I pause long enough to look and listen.

There is so much here, O Eternal One, so much You have made.
By the wise way in which You create, *riches and* creatures fill the earth.
Psalm 104:24 (The Voice)

Landgrove, Vermont

> Lately I have been challenged to practice Sabbath rest, and I realized that when I am refreshed and I am nourished, kindness seems to flow more naturally from me.

God of the waking heart, I am grateful this morning for Sabbath rest, for a day of peace that allows me to retreat from the work world to enjoy the gift of life's tiny treasures. I especially welcome the opportunity to be quiet where I can count my blessings and enter more deeply into your presence. Although I'm acutely aware of my own struggles and limitations, I come to You in trust that even when I experience failure, your grace reaches out to me, setting me free. Your Word reminds me that You rejoice when one of your children seeks You. I want to be one of those children.

Or suppose a woman has ten silver coins and loses one. Won't she light a lamp and sweep the entire house and search carefully until she finds it? And when she finds it, she will call in her friends and neighbors and say, 'Rejoice with me because I have found my lost coin.' In the same way, there is joy in the presence of God's angels when even one sinner repents. Luke 15:8-10 (NLT)

I can practice Sabbath rest by . . .

Shepherd of my soul, guide me through the coming hours as I journey together with You. May I be so aware of your presence that I can keep my focus on You and never lose my way. I pray that I might be open to the power and wisdom of your Holy Spirit directing my path and guiding my decisions as I lean on Jesus.

Be good to your servant, *GOD*;
   be as good as your Word.
Train me in good common sense;
   I'm thoroughly committed to living your way.
Before I learned to answer you, I wandered all over the place,
   but now I'm in step with your Word.
You are good, and the source of good;
   train me in your goodness.
Psalm 119:65-68 (The Message)

Today I lift this question to God . . .

OCTOBER 25

Great God of wonders, You are the creative artist who has designed the vista before me, both the inconceivable vastness of the galaxies of space and the tiny fingerprint of a newborn baby. You are the One who dressed the lilies of the field, the One who painted sunrises and sunsets, the One who counted every grain of sand and every breaking wave.

O God, I humble myself before You and bring to You my many feelings because they are a real part of who I am—my deep contentment, my burdens of anxiety, my soaring joy, my painful memories, and my unfinished dreams. I pray that You will meet me and comfort me in both my joys and my vulnerabilities.

The humble will see their God at work and be glad.
  Let all who seek God's help be encouraged.
Psalm 69:32 (NLT)

Cape Neddick, Maine

Dear Lord, I come to You, hoping that You might teach me once again how to let go, releasing in trust the people and situations that I often carry too closely. I keep learning the lesson that when I grip things tightly, I leave no space for You to work. So, into your loving hands I release my loved ones who seem determined to follow a path leading to inevitable pain; I entrust medical situations that I cannot change; I lift confusing decisions into the light of your understanding, so that I might discover both the clarity and capacity to make wise choices.

I offer to You all the concerns that trouble me this morning. And then, O Lord, envelop each situation and each person I have placed in your care with the deep, healing therapy of your love.

But I trust in your unfailing love.
  I will rejoice because you have rescued me.
I will sing to the LORD
  because he is good to me.
Psalm 13:5-6 (NLT)

Help me to release . . .

OCTOBER 27

Holy God, take away my obstacles so that I might hear You—your still, small voice that touches the center of my being, calling me to be the person You created me to be. Help me to be open to the sometimes comforting, sometimes challenging, often surprising ways You communicate with me. Help me to take just one more step with You. And the power of your presence will be my reward.

Then as I envision the week ahead, open my heart so that I can invite You to walk with me daily. Let this be my prayer: change my heart, O God; make me more like your Son, Jesus.

Because of this decision we don't evaluate people by what they have or how they look. We looked at the Messiah that way once and got it all wrong, as you know. We certainly don't look at him that way anymore. Now we look inside, and what we see is that anyone united with the Messiah gets a fresh start, is created new. The old life is gone; a new life burgeons! Look at it! All this comes from the God who settled the relationship between us and him, and then called us to settle our relationships with each other. God put the world square with himself through the Messiah, giving the world a fresh start by offering forgiveness of sins. God has given us the task of telling everyone what he is doing. We're Christ's representatives. God uses us to persuade men and women to drop their differences and enter into God's work of making things right between them. We're speaking for Christ himself now: Become friends with God; he's already a friend with you. 2 Corinthians 5:16-20 (The Message)

I can take one leap of faith to . . .

OCTOBER 28

O God of the ages, in many parts of this world, this is the season of autumn wonder. Your hand paints the valleys ablaze with beauty and the distant hills with the golden garlands of fall, and your glory shines through it all. Even here in Florida, I celebrate the subtle heralds of a new season—a morning of drier air, a soft breeze, and the promise of nature's turning. It is here that I settle into a tangible serenity. It is here that I reach out to You in praise, O Lord.

Sing out your thanks to the LORD;
*   sing praises to our God with a harp.*
He covers the heavens with clouds,
*   provides rain for the earth,*
*   and makes the grass grow in mountain pastures.*
Psalm 147:7-8 (NLT)

Dallas Divide, Colorado

> Prayer is where I bring all that I know of myself to all that I know of God.

O God of the whisper, You invite me to find solitude so that I can open my heart and quiet my mind to talk to You directly. I have all kinds of needs: for healing, forgiveness, encouragement, comfort, and guidance. It doesn't matter to You where I have been; You want me to seek You in prayer. In this sacred moment, I turn to You with simple words. Hear my prayers, O Lord. And then help me to rest in your holiness and listen with an open heart.

By day the LORD directs his love,
  at night his song is with me—
  a prayer to the God of my life.
Psalm 42:8 (NIV)

If I am fully present with You in prayer today, I will . . .

Precious Lord, You have reminded me of my need to center my spirit deeply in a place of trust in You. Free me from my restless worries and my preoccupation with events over which I have no control. You have invited me to be still and dwell in You without fear, to simply rest and trust. O Lord, as You once spoke peace to the wind and the waves, whisper your calm over my heart so that I might wait silently and learn to enjoy the gift of your companionship. And then, O Lord, continue your re-creation in me, taking me from fearful to confident, from shaken to courageous, and from unprotected to sheltered in your mercy.

The LORD keeps watch over you as you come and go,
both now and forever.
Psalm 121:8 (NLT)

What parts of myself need transformation?

All Things Bright And Beautiful

Refrain:
All things bright and beautiful,
All creatures great and small,
All things wise and wonderful,
The Lord God made them all.

Each little flower that opens,
Each little bird that sings,
He made their glowing colours,
He made their tiny wings.

The purple-headed mountain,
The river running by,
The sunset and the morning,
That brightens up the sky;

The cold wind in the winter,
The pleasant summer sun,
The ripe fruits in the garden,
He made them every one;

The tall trees in the greenwood,
The meadows for our play,
The rushes by the water,
To gather every day;

He gave us eyes to see them,
And lips that we might tell
How great is God Almighty,
Who has made all things well.

Cecil Frances Alexander, 1848

Dallas Divide, Colorado

OCTOBER 31

Lord of all time, your power illuminates the stars of the galaxies, and in much the same way, your love ignites my life with a holy purpose in my world. O God of wisdom, I seek guidance far beyond anything I might comprehend on my own. I have truly discovered that everything I offer to the world comes from the overflow of your great wisdom and grace.

My child, listen to what I say,
  and treasure my commands.
Tune your ears to wisdom,
  and concentrate on understanding.
Cry out for insight,
  and ask for understanding.
Search for them as you would for silver;
  seek them like hidden treasures.
Then you will understand what it means to fear the LORD,
  and you will gain knowledge of God.
For the LORD grants wisdom!
  From his mouth come knowledge and understanding.
He grants a treasure of common sense to the honest.
  He is a shield to those who walk with integrity.
He guards the paths of the just
  and protects those who are faithful to him.
Then you will understand what is right, just, and fair,
  and you will find the right way to go.
For wisdom will enter your heart,
  and knowledge will fill you with joy.
Wise choices will watch over you.
  Understanding will keep you safe.
Proverbs 2:1-11 NLT

NOVEMBER 1

Yahweh, Lord of creation, as the winds of autumn gently scatter the leaves across yards, so may the breath of your Spirit move me. Come and blow away the dust of complacency in any part of my life that makes my world look bleak. Grant me the vision to see each day as a gift from You, whatever form it might take. May the winds of your Spirit fill my lungs with new life, fresh and breezy as this November morning. Free me, ready me, to live a life renewed in You.

Don't lie to one another. You're done with that old life. It's like a filthy set of ill-fitting clothes you've stripped off and put in the fire. Now you're dressed in a new wardrobe. Every item of your new way of life is custom-made by the Creator, with his label on it. All the old fashions are now obsolete. Words like Jewish and non-Jewish, religious and irreligious, insider and outsider, uncivilized and uncouth, slave and free, mean nothing. From now on everyone is defined by Christ, everyone is included in Christ. Colossians 3:9-11 (The Message)

River Falls, Wisconsin

NOVEMBER 2

This cool, fall morning I had a flashback to my father at Lake Tahoe. Every morning he would go outside on the porch and breathe in the fresh air as if to announce, "This is the day that the Lord has made. Let us rejoice and be glad in it."

Abba, my God, I give thanks for all the ways You offer me a perfect father's love: unconditional, faithful, strong, and constant. When I'm open to the power of your Holy Spirit, You fill me again with faith that is vibrant and full. Send me out today with a sense of purpose so that I might be your enthusiastic partner in this world, offering grace upon grace so that others can witness the abundant life You offer.

Give thanks to the God of heaven.
   His faithful love endures forever.
Psalm 136:26 (NLT)

My life's purpose includes . . .

NOVEMBER 3

O God of this day and all moments in time, I am ruled by clock and calendar and can barely comprehend the mystery of eternal life. Limited by my own understanding, I sometimes struggle to grasp the limitless possibilities You offer to me. You reveal the depth of your love for me in Jesus and remind me each day that You also care about the details of my life. In Jesus, You showed me your love for each person—for the weary, for those who were ill, for those without direction—You embraced them all.

Hear my prayers for people I know in desperate situations who cry out for your limitless love and hope. Embrace me and each one who seeks You today, offering hope for the deepest desires that flow from within—for yours is the Kingdom that never dies and the love that never ends.

He tends his flock like a shepherd:
  He gathers the lambs in his arms
and carries them close to his heart;
  he gently leads those that have young.
Isaiah 40:11 (NIV)

What is my deepest desire?

NOVEMBER 4

God of the created cosmos, I give thanks for the wonder of being alive on this most amazing day. I am grateful for beauty in all its forms—for the wide canopy of brilliance that is named sky and for a single butterfly circling the golden grapevines. Thank you for your Word that strikes my soul with undeserved mercy and the gracious kindness of authentic forgiveness. This day and every day, I pray that my heart would be awakened and my eyes opened to the wonders that lead to spontaneous celebration.

Then the earth will yield its harvests,
*   and God, our God, will richly bless us.*
Psalm 67:6 (NLT)

Napa Valley, California

NOVEMBER 5

> "Prayer is a very dangerous business. For all the benefits it offers of growing closer to God, it carries with it one great element of risk—the possibility of change." Emilie Griffin, author

God of my heart, it is the spirit of Jesus Christ, his living and dying and new life, that compel me to be here in prayer and call me to trust that I can speak my soul's desires. I know that You listen to my voice and my heart. When I leave this time of prayer with You, do not let me remain unchanged. Teach me to embody your grace and offer the gift of your peace to others, through the power of my Lord, Jesus Christ.

Now may the God of peace, who brought back from the dead our Lord Jesus, the great shepherd of the sheep, by the blood of the eternal covenant, make you complete in everything good so that you may do his will, working among us that which is pleasing in his sight, through Jesus Christ, to whom be the glory forever and ever. Amen. Hebrews 13:20-21 (NRSV)

If I could change anything in my life it would be . . .

NOVEMBER 6

Blessed Lord, thank you for helping me make the shift from rushing around to simply being quiet in your presence. In worship, when I discover the delight of resting in sacred space, surrounded by countless others who desire the same connection, your words have a richer meaning. Where two or three are gathered, your presence is known in a mysterious way. Thank you for weekly gifts of worship where word and silence and melody spill into my soul, bringing me a taste of your Kingdom here on earth.

Praise the LORD.
Praise God in his sanctuary;
   praise him in his mighty heavens.
Praise him for his acts of power;
   praise him for his surpassing greatness.
Praise him with the sounding of the trumpet,
   praise him with the harp and lyre,
praise him with timbrel and dancing,
   praise him with the strings and pipe,
praise him with the clash of cymbals,
   praise him with resounding cymbals.
Psalm 150:1-5 (NIV)

In worship I am drawn into God's presence by . . .

Redwoods, California

NOVEMBER 7

The magnificent California redwoods are the tallest trees on earth and can live to be two thousand years old. But they have one major weakness: their shallow root system. Standing alone, a redwood is doomed. However, they can survive for millennia by growing close together in a cathedral grove where the shallow roots intermingle in a support system that can withstand any force of nature. Protected by the giants of the cathedral, the generations of redwoods sprout and grow. In the same way, none of us is intended to live alone but to be woven together with others in the Body of Christ, to offer strength and nourishment to our world.

O Compassionate Lord, You remind me often that life is more than worrying about my own life. It is reaching out to others with the grace You have offered to me. Grant me the willingness to embrace the ones who are difficult for me to love. I pray for the ones who want to let go of a problem but cannot seem to release it into your care; the ones whose hearts are pounding with stress; the ones who have created a wall of protection against hurt; the ones who battle daily to forgive one near to them; and the ones I know who carry a quiet grief alone.
I pray for a heart that knows generosity of spirit so that I would have the time, space, and resources to offer daily, quiet acts of service.

Real wisdom, God's wisdom, begins with a holy life and is characterized by getting along with others. It is gentle and reasonable, overflowing with mercy and blessings, not hot one day and cold the next, not two-faced. You can develop a healthy, robust community that lives right with God and enjoy its results only if you do the hard work of getting along with each other, treating each other with dignity and honor. James 3:17-18 (The Message)

NOVEMBER 8

O Lord, grant me quietness of mind so that I might know your presence. Grant me softness of heart so that I might be moved by the needs I see in the world. Grant me strength of will so that I might approach every situation with the attitude that I might be a conduit of your grace. Help me to dwell in the peace of your presence now, my life mirroring the richness of your grace. Strengthen me to do your work and your will through Jesus Christ, my Lord.

In view of all this, make every effort to respond to God's promises. Supplement your faith with a generous provision of moral excellence, and moral excellence with knowledge, and knowledge with self-control, and self-control with patient endurance, and patient endurance with godliness, and godliness with brotherly affection, and brotherly affection with love for everyone.
The more you grow like this, the more productive and useful you will be in your knowledge of our Lord Jesus Christ. But those who fail to develop in this way are shortsighted or blind, forgetting that they have been cleansed from their old sins. 2 Peter 1:5-9 (NLT)

What work do I want to accomplish for God?

NOVEMBER 9

Precious Lord, I invite You to take my hand and lead me to rest in your presence. Remind me again this day that my heart will forever be restless until it finds a resting place in You. Quiet my harried heart long enough to surprise me with the joy of your presence—loving me, forgiving me, and making me whole again.

You will show me the way of life,
  granting me the joy of your presence
  and the pleasures of living with you forever.
Psalm 16:11 (NLT)

Where do I discover simple joy?

NOVEMBER 10

God of the ages, You scatter the darkness of night with the dawn's glow, casting your brilliance as a sacrament of hope. You meet me in every moment, but especially in the still spaces, where the clutter of my soul gives way to the serenity of embodied prayer. I discover that I am breathing more deeply, seeing more clearly, resting more fully in You. In countless ways, You are teaching me to cherish the bits of abundant life scattered throughout my days.

I long, yes, I faint with longing
  to enter the courts of the LORD.
With my whole being, body and soul,
  I will shout joyfully to the living God.
Psalm 84:2 (NLT)

Brenda Berry

NOVEMBER 11

O Lord of all, on this Veterans Day, I pray for those who have served our country with courage and dignity, especially those who are now wounded in body or in spirit and need your grace in special ways. I pray for all those held captive by behavior or by circumstances. I pray for each one who is engulfed in

grief or sadness,

worry or anxiety,

disappointment or betrayal,

trusting You to take them from my heart and wrap them in your grace. I know that You will transform their lives according to your will and in your time. Lord, in this moment I offer You my prayers for those situations I now surrender into your eternal arms. I pray for breakthroughs of unexpected grace in the name of my Lord, Jesus Christ.

Be prepared. You're up against far more than you can handle on your own. Take all the help you can get, every weapon God has issued, so that when it's all over but the shouting you'll still be on your feet. Truth, righteousness, peace, faith, and salvation are more than words. Learn how to apply them. You'll need them throughout your life. God's Word is an indispensable weapon. In the same way, prayer is essential in this ongoing warfare. Pray hard and long. Pray for your brothers and sisters. Keep your eyes open. Keep each other's spirits up so that no one falls behind or drops out. Ephesians 6:13-18 (The Message)

Today, my prayers extend to . . .

NOVEMBER 12

God of abundant life, I am reminded that when I seek You, your love can change my apathy into renewed passion for living. I celebrate that You free me from the chains that bind me to my old life. You offer to reach out to turn my tears into dancing and my sorrow into joy. I am humbled to know that You, the Lord of the universe, pour out your Spirit on me when I need You. As I seek fellowship with others, I pray that each one of us be filled with hope for the future. I know that your Spirit moves to rejuvenate and empower us as we go out to be your ambassadors of grace in the world.

And now, dear brothers and sisters, one final thing. Fix your thoughts on what is true, and honorable, and right, and pure, and lovely, and admirable. Think about things that are excellent and worthy of praise. Keep putting into practice all you learned and received from me—everything you heard from me and saw me doing. Then the God of peace will be with you. Philippians 4:8-9 (NLT)

I want to experience freedom from . . .

NOVEMBER 13

Dear God, deep within me is a longing to live with the power and the purpose that You alone can provide. I am so grateful that your forgiving touch is as faithful as the setting of the sun each evening, centering me once again in You. I yearn for a deeper connection with You but have sought comfort in many empty places. And so I turn to You, bringing whatever has been a struggle in my life into your mercy and your grace for redirection.

Have mercy on me, O God,
*   because of your unfailing love.*
Because of your great compassion,
*   blot out the stain of my sins.*
Wash me clean from my guilt.
*   Purify me from my sin.*
Psalm 51:1-2 (NLT)

Danby, Vermont

NOVEMBER 14

O Lord, You have searched my heart and You know me, yet my heart is forever wandering. With the temptation to take the easier way, with the small choices I make that strip me of my integrity, I often evade You, the One who knows me by name. Give me the willingness to approach You with a heart wide open to your healing grace. May my eyes be opened to those conflicts hidden deep within my heart that You want to show me. And then, sweep them away with your healing touch and forgiving strength through Christ my Lord.

No test or temptation that comes your way is beyond the course of what others have had to face. All you need to remember is that God will never let you down; he'll never let you be pushed past your limit; he'll always be there to help you come through it. 1 Corinthians 10:13 (The Message)

Which conflicts do I need to offer to God?

NOVEMBER 15

Loving God, I am reminded of how easily my commitment to You can fade with a shift in my emotions—yet your faithfulness and love remain rock-solid. O Lord, I am struck by how humbly your Son came into this world and was laid in a manger. He worked for years as a simple carpenter. In his last week on earth he traveled to a dusty city, riding on a donkey. I am reminded by his example of another path—a different way to invest my life, to be ready and willing in service and in sacrifice. When life's struggles threaten to sear my soul or suffering strips me of hope, You are the source of my faith and courage, for You are the Author of new life.

Jesus answered, "I am the way and the truth and the life. No one comes to the Father except through me." John 14:6 (NIV)

I struggle being humble enough to . . .

NOVEMBER 16

O God of all creation, it is so easy to see your beauty in puffs of tangerine clouds marching against a darkening sky or in the silvery reflections of palm fronds dancing in the wind. But, Lord, in this season of gratitude, can I dare to see your face in the dark situations that find their way into my life? Can I glimpse your holiness in the midst of life's confusing circumstances? O Lord, I understand that gratitude unlocks the fullness of life, so help me to look for your fingerprints wherever I might be, trusting ultimately that You will make sense of it all.

But you are a chosen people, a royal priesthood, a holy nation, God's special possession, that you may declare the praises of him who called you out of darkness into his wonderful light. Once you were not a people, but now you are the people of God; once you had not received mercy, but now you have received mercy. 1 Peter 2:9-10 (NIV)

Anguilla

Bill Bohlke

NOVEMBER 17

God of grace, You love me as I am. But your love is so great, You patiently challenge me and teach me new truths about how to live a more abundant life. When I experience the power of music stirring my spirit and the impact of your Word on my mind and heart, I turn to You with the hope of a renewal that might change not only me but all my relationships. Empower me and launch me into service in your Kingdom here on earth. May the people I meet today feel touched by your presence within me.

And let the peace that comes from Christ rule in your hearts. For as members of one body you are called to live in peace. And always be thankful.
Let the message about Christ, in all its richness, fill your lives. Teach and counsel each other with all the wisdom he gives. Sing psalms and hymns and spiritual songs to God with thankful hearts. Colossians 3:15-16 (NLT)

God has empowered me to ...

NOVEMBER 18

Dear God, in the midst of my soul's winter, I have to admit that I sometimes wonder if You are really trustworthy, if I can truly count on your goodness. Then, I'm reassured when I discover that some of the heroes of faith felt doubt and anger, too. You always invite my sincere cries, offering me soul therapy when I come to You in honest prayer. It is only in my vulnerability that You release me from my dark fears, leading me into the light of renewed faith. It is only in my surrender that You free me from the prisons of my own making. Remind me that the answers to my dilemmas lie in seeking advice from You, the God of all wisdom.

For I am the LORD your God
who takes hold of your right hand
and says to you, Do not fear;
I will help you.
Isaiah 41:13 (NIV)

Which fears keep me from living an abundant life with God?

NOVEMBER 19

Author Anne Lamott said, "The most honest prayers of our hearts begin with the single word, 'Help,' but continue with, 'Thank you.'"

Ever-present Lord, as I approach the hurried sprint that sometimes defines the holiday season, help me to appreciate the gift of anticipation—for I have lost the ability to wait, to cherish the moment, to embrace uncertainty, and so often, to live by faith. I blow through my days at such a dizzying speed that I rarely stop long enough to consider and give thanks to You, the source of all my blessings. So, as I enter this season of Thanksgiving, I pray that gratitude and peace would increasingly become the way I mark each day.

But let the godly rejoice.
  Let them be glad in God's presence.
  Let them be filled with joy.
Psalm 68:3 (NLT)

Versailles, Kentucky

NOVEMBER 20

God of mercy, I am learning to trust in your steadfast faithfulness even when I cannot see it or feel it. So I turn to You with my prayers that encompass so many people whose needs reside in my heart. In this holiday season, I pray
for families separated by miles;
for youth struggling to find purpose;
for loved ones burdened by health challenges;
for the countless ones who need the tenderness of a word or deed
that communicates that they matter in this world.
Thank you for the opportunity to use the gifts You have given to me to impact my world with compassion and justice. In this season of giving, I pray that You would lead me to be generous in grace, mercy, and peace as I share myself and my resources, entrusting myself into your care.

See that no one pays back evil for evil, but always try to do good to each other and to all people.
Always be joyful. Never stop praying. Be thankful in all circumstances, for this is God's will for you who belong to Christ Jesus.
1 Thessalonians 5:15-18 (NLT)

Which continuing struggles in my life do I need to release to God?

NOVEMBER 21

God of wonder, I am filled with the joy of being alive today. I ponder all the ways You have been at work in my life—for the moments of laughter blasting through the yoke of weariness and for the joyful explosion of melody that stirs my spirit.

Help me to sink deep into the knowledge that whatever my relationship is with You, You hold me in your everlasting arms. You encourage me to take one more step of faith towards a life committed to your will and your ways. As I grow in faith, help me to pave the way for your Kingdom with my prayer and praise, with my service and love, until the very stones cry out at the coming of your new creation through Jesus Christ, my Lord.

When he came near the place where the road goes down the Mount of Olives, the whole crowd of disciples began joyfully to praise God in loud voices for all the miracles they had seen:

"Blessed is the king who comes in the name of the Lord!"

"Peace in heaven and glory in the highest!"

Some of the Pharisees in the crowd said to Jesus, "Teacher, rebuke your disciples!"

"I tell you," he replied, "if they keep quiet, the stones will cry out."
Luke 19:37-40 (NIV)

A new step of faith for me would be . . .

NOVEMBER 22

God of all blessings, I pause to give thanks. Thank you for the mystery of creation: the songs of birds, the sound of children at play, and the tenderness of a grandparent's smile. Each new dawn is filled with infinite possibilities and ordinary miracles, and each is a gift from your hand. You remind me daily to open the eyes of my heart to see the message of your love poured out in Jesus Christ.

There, in the presence of the LORD your God, you and your families shall eat and shall rejoice in everything you have put your hand to, because the LORD your God has blessed you. Deuteronomy 12:7 (NIV)

Brenda Berry

NOVEMBER 23

Living God, the freshness of the morning breeze fills me with new life, making me feel as vibrant as this November morning. I am grateful for your constancy in my life, for your pursuing love and redeeming grace in Jesus Christ, my Lord. During this season, I thank You for the blessings of the year, for times of health and plenty. I am also grateful for strength in my days of difficulties, comfort in my nights of sorrow, and guidance on every shadowy path of my journey. You are the source of hope because Jesus Christ has conquered the power of death and gives me the promise of eternity.

For the LORD your God is living among you.
  He is a mighty savior.
He will take delight in you with gladness.
  With his love, he will calm all your fears.
  He will rejoice over you with joyful songs.
Zephaniah 3:17 (NLT)

When I count my blessings, I include . . .

O bountiful God, I worship You with a heart overflowing with thanksgiving.
For all the blessings of the land, I give You my gratitude:

for all good and beautiful gifts that come from your hand,
for food that nourishes my body,
for the windswept expanse of ocean blue,
for mountain ranges that crown this land with majesty.

I turn to You, thankful that your faithfulness stretches across the heavens,
and your love spans the farthest reaches of the stars.

Come, Ye Thankful People, Come

Come, ye thankful people, come,
raise the song of harvest home;
all is safely gathered in,
ere the winter storms begin.
God our Maker doth provide
for our wants to be supplied;
come to God's own temple, come,
raise the song of harvest home.
Henry Alford, 1844

What strikes wonder in my soul?

NOVEMBER 25

Giver of all grace, I am blessed by the special people who have walked with me in all my life stages, enriching me with moments of ordinary tenderness. And You have gifted me with a world full of breathtaking beauty. You meet me here on holy ground where the golden sun illuminates the morning around me. Help me to learn, as your disciples did, about what it means to live fully in your Kingdom—to abide completely in this moment, aware and alive, celebrating who You are and what You have done for me. You sow the seeds of freedom and joy within the hearts of each one willing to trust in You.

With every sun's rising, *surprise us* with Your love,
   satisfy us with Your kindness.
Then we will sing with joy and celebrate every day we are alive.
Psalm 90:14 (The Voice)

Jupiter, Florida   Laurie Bohlke

NOVEMBER 26

Merciful God, in this season of Thanksgiving, I pause to contemplate one by one the gifts of grace that I treasure: the blessing of my freedoms; the wonder that hides behind a child's simple prayer; the tenderness that shines through the eyes of loved ones; the warmth of familiar voices reaching out over the miles; and the compassionate grace that enfolds me when I recognize your sacred presence blessing my life. You whisper to me in the most commonplace events of each day. You invite me to lift up the cries of my heart, entrusting the ones I love to You, for You care for them with an everlasting love.

So, teach me to live thankfully, not only on this day, but every day, recognizing that true joy grows from a life rooted in contentment. And strengthen me for the work that You have prepared for me to do—to brighten this world through your love and peace.

Oh come, let us sing to the LORD;
let us make a joyful noise to the rock of our salvation!
Let us come into his presence with thanksgiving;
let us make a joyful noise to him with songs of praise!
Psalm 95:1-2 (ESV)

God whispers to me in . . .

NOVEMBER 27

Remind me, O Lord, that it is sometimes in the single note of a bird's call, the spark of a smile in the eyes of a total stranger, or the unexpected simple faith of a child's prayer that I experience your presence anew. Grant me eyes of wonder to see your presence in all the events of each day unfolding before me. Then gift me with the ability to live that day with expectancy, eager for the mysteries You will unwrap for me, grateful for the richness of all of life's tapestry.

O LORD, our Lord, your majestic name fills the earth!
Your glory is higher than the heavens.
You have taught children and infants
to tell of your strength,
silencing your enemies
and all who oppose you.
When I look at the night sky and see the work of your fingers—
the moon and the stars you set in place—
what are mere mortals that you should think about them,
human beings that you should care for them?
Yet you made them only a little lower than God
and crowned them with glory and honor.
Psalm 8:1-5 (NLT)

I experience God's presence most deeply when . . .

NOVEMBER 28

Lord of all creation, the third star in the evening sky ushered me into the peace of your presence last evening, and then You gifted me with a night of much-needed rest. Thank you for the peace and contentment at the heart of lingering in your presence. Abba God, help me to remember what is most important in life and then help me to walk more slowly, live more simply, and love more boldly. Allow my heart the space to know You and serve You with gratitude and gladness.

In peace I will lie down and sleep,
  for you alone, O LORD, will keep me safe.
Psalm 4:8 (NLT)

Churchill, Canada

NOVEMBER 29

I love this quote from author Emilie Griffin: "In prayer we open ourselves to the chance that God will do something with us that we had not intended."

God of all glory, this year more than ever, I need Advent, the time for slowing down and reflection on the gift of Jesus Christ to our world. Help me to acknowledge a longing for connection deep in my soul. When I am honest with myself, I sense that something is missing, and I suspect it's about You, Lord. I know that You are not missing from my life, but I am missing the awareness that You are here, ready and willing to break into my days to surprise, bless, and encourage. Be with me, but more importantly, help me to be with You, to make space for You to come and dwell in the crowded inn of my life.

Come close to God, and God will come close to you. Wash your hands, you sinners; purify your hearts, for your loyalty is divided between God and the world. Let there be tears for what you have done. Let there be sorrow and deep grief. Let there be sadness instead of laughter, and gloom instead of joy. Humble yourselves before the Lord, and he will lift you up in honor.
James 4:8-10 (NLT)

I can make space for God by . . .

NOVEMBER 30

O God of unfathomable goodness, I pause in the midst of the uncertainties of these times, especially the crises that encircle the planet, and pray for those who are carrying burdens that are heavier than they can manage on their own. O Lord, help each one to know, even in the midst of problems and pain, a glimpse of your radiant glory, a window into your world. Help each one to see your face, sense the mystery in all things, and walk with You through it all. Bring each one who seeks You closer to You in the challenging times and the calmer moments. O Lord, I pray for generosity of spirit, so that I would look beyond my own desires to have the time, space, and resources to offer your grace to others in daily quiet acts of service.

Don't be afraid, for I am with you.
  Don't be discouraged, for I am your God.
I will strengthen you and help you.
  I will hold you up with my victorious right hand.
Isaiah 41:10 (NLT)

A random act of kindness might be . . .

DECEMBER 1

I love Christmas, but I get caught up in the stress of it all. Every year I sit beneath the twinkle lights for my morning prayer and remember Lois Matthews, who was an older, wiser woman and one of the dear saints at Troy United Church of Christ. Years ago, when I was a young pastor, she shared with me these words of wisdom: "Try to get all possible preparations done for Christmas by St. Thomas Day" (which was traditionally December 21st). It's great advice because it gives me time to prepare my heart for the spiritual depth of Christmas.

O Lord of this wondrous season, peace often resides in the most surprising places—in the twinkle lights sparkling in trees, in the sweet fragrance of pine, in the candles glimmering in the twilight. I give thanks for my community of faith and for spiritual gifts found, not under a brightly adorned tree but in the hearts of my friends. Help me not only to enjoy the traditions but to wait for the startling newness of Christ's presence awakened in me again.

God has given each of you a gift from his great variety of spiritual gifts. Use them well to serve one another. Do you have the gift of speaking? Then speak as though God himself were speaking through you. Do you have the gift of helping others? Do it with all the strength and energy that God supplies. Then everything you do will bring glory to God through Jesus Christ. All glory and power to him forever and ever! Amen. 1 Peter 4:10-11 (NLT)

Vail, Colorado

DECEMBER 2

This day, Precious Lord, I have come to rest a while with You, to wait for the gift of your sacred presence reaching out to meet me. I know that You are always communicating with me in the ordinary experiences of life and that, in the midst of earthly time, You are giving me precious glimpses of eternity. Lift high my spirit, so that I might look beyond the limits of my horizons to glimpse the wide expanses of your eternal vision. Let my life reflect the hope and joy and power of life in Jesus Christ, my Savior.

Your eternal word, O LORD,
stands firm in heaven.
Your faithfulness extends to every generation,
as enduring as the earth you created.
Psalm 119:89-90 (NLT)

Yesterday I recognized God's presence in . . .

DECEMBER 3

Emmanuel, God with us, remind me again of what this season is about—the promise that your love reached out from heaven on that first Christmas to touch all people with your peace and joy. You have repeated that message every day since. Calm me; slow my thoughts. Help me to remember that You gave your Son to the world, and your gift is the heart of all of the Christmas celebrations. It will not be through the tinsel or the decorations or the presents that I sense You but in those eternal instants where You reach out through a word or a wink or a silent moment to embrace me with your presence.

For God so loved the world that he gave his one and only Son, that whoever believes in him shall not perish but have eternal life. John 3:16 (NIV)

I feel God's embrace when . . .

DECEMBER 4

Merciful God, I join my heart with the many who need your presence in the days ahead. Pour out your strength on all who are facing difficult situations: the ones who are afraid of letting go of control and so find it difficult to trust You, and the ones who are running from You and everything that is good in their lives. Shine your compassionate light on those seeking wisdom as they make their decisions. O Lord, I surrender each concern and each situation to You, asking You to bless each troubled soul with your healing, reconciling, and comforting presence. Above all else, I pray that I would put You at the center of all my celebrations, through Him who came to us, Jesus Christ our Lord.

You, LORD, are my lamp;
  the LORD turns my darkness into light.
2 Samuel 22:29 (NIV)

Jupiter, Florida   Bill Bohlke

DECEMBER 5

O God, whose glory encircles my life, I know I am in the presence of your Son and my Lord, Jesus Christ. I have glimpsed your spirit touching a life here, filling another with glory there, and so I come before You today in awe and gratitude. Gracious God, I recognize that all of my real inspiration, all of my depths of understanding, and all of my renewed life are the fruit of your amazing Spirit, and I cannot help giving my praise and thanks to You.

But what happens when we live God's way? He brings gifts into our lives, much the same way that fruit appears in an orchard—things like affection for others, exuberance about life, serenity. We develop a willingness to stick with things, a sense of compassion in the heart, and a conviction that a basic holiness permeates things and people. We find ourselves involved in loyal commitments, not needing to force our way in life, able to marshal and direct our energies wisely. . . Galatians 5:22-23a (The Message)

Today I celebrate these new wonders in my life:

DECEMBER 6

Living God, I anticipate gathering at your Communion table. The gift of your Son reaches through the ages to meet me here. I am hungry for what truly satisfies and thirsty for your refreshing witness in my life. Prepare my heart this Advent season to receive You in a fresh new way as I release myself to You. Surprise me with the countless ways You reveal your presence to me, often through unexpected situations and messengers. Then help me to be open to take the next step of discipleship.

As they approached the village to which they were going, Jesus continued on as if he were going farther. But they urged him strongly, "Stay with us, for it is nearly evening; the day is almost over." So he went in to stay with them.
When he was at the table with them, he took bread, gave thanks, broke it and began to give it to them. Then their eyes were opened and they recognized him, and he disappeared from their sight. They asked each other, "Were not our hearts burning within us while he talked with us on the road and opened the Scriptures to us?" Luke 24:28-32 (NIV)

I can prepare my heart to receive Christ this season by . . .

DECEMBER 7

O Lord of joyous sound, choruses of praise erupt all over creation celebrating your goodness—in brass bands heralding the birth of a King, in children's giggles in a season made for them, and soon in the celebration of the angel choruses. I give You thanks for the carols of the Christmas season and the delight they bring. O Lord, I am grateful for all the amazing graces of life, laughter, and song. Thank you for the blessings of friends and family—especially for children.

For I will pour out water to quench your thirst
*   and to irrigate your parched fields.*
And I will pour out my Spirit on your descendants,
*   and my blessing on your children.*
Isaiah 44:3 (NLT)

DECEMBER 8

God of all hopefulness, today I am acutely aware of the gift of being alive and joyous and free because I am loved by You. This time of quiet prayer opens the windows of my soul, allowing the whisper of your Holy Spirit to penetrate my own defenses. When I pause before You in honest reflection, I realize that I have squandered far too many of the moments in my days with a life only half lived. God of today, I pray that You will awaken me from rushing through everyday moments as if life is a race to be completed in record time, rather than as lingering moments to be savored with joy-tinged wonder.

I take joy in doing your will, my God,
  for your instructions are written on my heart.
Psalm 40:8 (NLT)

I need your grace in this situation today . . .

DECEMBER 9

O God who hears me and beckons to me, You reach through the crush of Christmastime to embrace me, one whose longing life needs your touch. Awaken my spirit to your presence this day. In this season of the star, let your hand hold me and heal me. Let your love come to me. Let the promise of the child of Bethlehem drive away all that has hardened my heart. Humble me, O Lord, so that I might know that even when small miracles happen, they come from your mighty hand. Grant me the spirit of repentance so that my heart can turn again to You. Show me how to love others, even my enemies, leading me to forgive others as freely as Jesus did. May my eyes be opened, Lord, so that I can follow You.

For you are all children of God through faith in Christ Jesus. And all who have been united with Christ in baptism have put on Christ, like putting on new clothes. There is no longer Jew or Gentile, slave or free, male and female. For you are all one in Christ Jesus. Galatians 3:26-28 (NLT)

The last time I experienced a small miracle was . . .

DECEMBER 10

Be my Comforter, O Wonderful Counselor. As I struggle through a season focused on joy and celebration, a shroud of sadness blankets my spirit. When mountains seem to block my way to living fully, be my mighty God, able to do abundantly more than I can ask or think. When trust comes very slowly, if at all, help me to see that You are the everlasting God, faithful and trustworthy in everything. When my anxious worry casts a pall over any attempts at living in faith, be my Prince of Peace. As I anticipate the days ahead, I pray for your Spirit to walk before me, shining a light on my path to guide me and empower me to be your faithful servant.

God blesses those who patiently endure testing and temptation. Afterward they will receive the crown of life that God has promised to those who love him.
James 1:12 (NLT)

Vail, Colorado

DECEMBER 11

O Lord of all creation, I am grateful for those moments when I experience the incredible wonder of living—for morning stillness where all creation seems to stir, shake sleep away, and awaken to a fresh day of promise. It is in those seconds of grace-filled awe that I find myself amazed and grateful, and I am led back to You.

Praise the LORD, you angels,
  you mighty ones who carry out his plans,
  listening for each of his commands.
Yes, praise the LORD, you armies of angels
  who serve him and do his will!
Praise the LORD, everything he has created,
  everything in all his kingdom.
Let all that I am praise the LORD.
Psalm 103:20-22 (NLT)

Lord, this morning I want to greet You with . . .

DECEMBER 12

In the midst of all of my preparations, O Lord, give me a seeking heart as a reminder of the deeper mysteries of this season: that You, the Creator of the Universe, chose to enter this world as an infant, poor and vulnerable, yet destined to change the course of all human history—and each of our lives.

Keep me alert, waiting for Christmas to arrive anew in the hearts of each one watching for a glimpse of hope or a guiding hand. Come and dwell within me so that I might open my life to provide a guiding light and place of refuge to others as I celebrate the birth of your Son.

Guide me in your truth and teach me,
  for you are God my Savior,
  and my hope is in you all day long.
Psalm 25:5 (NIV)

Where is my seeking heart taking me?

DECEMBER 13

Blessed Lord, during this season of swirling activity, remind me of the need for inner quiet where I can reflect on the wilderness places in my life that You long to reach. Wherever I find myself, meet me with the power of your grace and truth so that I might seek You with the perseverance of the wise men. So, I come to you, Prince of Peace, and thank you for the brief silence of these moments, for I believe that in the peace, the child of Bethlehem draws near. To paraphrase "O Little Town of Bethlehem": "O Lord, impart to my heart the blessings of your heaven. Create in me a silence and in this silence dwell, so come to me, abide with me, my Lord Emmanuel."

> O holy Child of Bethlehem,
> Descend to us, we pray;
> Cast out our sins and enter in,
> Be born to us today.
> We hear the Christmas angels
> The great glad tidings tell:
> Oh, come to us, abide with us,
> Our Lord Emmanuel!
>> *Philip Brooks, 1868*

Danby, Vermont

DECEMBER 14

O Lord of the wounded soul, in this season of the impossible-come-true, I pray that those whose hearts are heavy would find relief, those who are carrying anger might find it possible to forgive, and those who dream impossible dreams might see them unfold before their eyes. My honest prayer is that You would walk with me in this season so that I might open my life to provide a sanctuary for one person in need, in the name of Jesus Christ, my Lord.

And God will generously provide all you need. Then you will always have everything you need and plenty left over to share with others. 2 Corinthians 9:8 (NLT)

What could I share with others today?

DECEMBER 15

In this season that celebrates peace, I remember the words attributed to St. Francis:

Lord, Make Me an Instrument of Your Peace

O Lord, make me an instrument of your peace;
Where there is hatred, let me sow love;
Where there is injury, pardon;
Where there is discord, harmony;
Where there is error, truth;
Where there is doubt, faith;
Where there is despair, hope;
Where there is darkness, light;
And where there is sadness, joy.

O Divine Master, grant that I might not so much seek
To be consoled as to console;
To be understood as to understand;
To be loved, as to love
For it is in giving that we receive;
It is in pardoning that we are pardoned;
And it is in dying that we are born to eternal life.
Lord, let this be such a day for me.

Accept one another, then, just as Christ accepted you, in order to bring praise to God.
Romans 15:7 (NIV)

Where do I yearn to witness peace unfolding in my world?

DECEMBER 16

During this coming week, Lord, at times I know I will not be able to sense your presence or be aware of your nearness. When I am lonely, I trust You to be my companion; when I am anxious, I trust You to remind me to rest in your presence; when I am rushed and running, I trust You to still my soul; and even, O Lord, when I forget You, I trust that You will never forget me.

If I ride the wings of the morning,
*   if I dwell by the farthest oceans,*
even there your hand will guide me,
*   and your strength will support me.*
Psalm 139:9-10 (NLT)

Long-eared owl, Colorado

DECEMBER 17

Thank you, Gracious Lord, for the return of the wondrous magic of the Christmas season that brings its own sweet joy. In the hush of these few moments, I remember the beauty of Christmas and the familiar carols that remind me of that great miracle—You created the universe, yet humbled yourself to come as an infant to lie in the embrace of his mother's arms. O God, before such mystery, I pause in wonder and praise.

Away in a Manger

Away in a manger, no crib for a bed,
The little Lord Jesus laid down his sweet head.
The stars in the sky looked down where he lay,
The little Lord Jesus asleep in the hay.

The cattle are lowing, the baby awakes,
But little Lord Jesus no crying he makes.
I love Thee, Lord Jesus, look down from the sky
And stay by my cradle til morning is nigh.

Be near me, Lord Jesus, I ask Thee to stay
Close by me forever, and love me, I pray.
Bless all the dear children in thy tender care,
And take us to heaven, to live with Thee there.
Unknown author

My favorite Christmas moment is . . .

DECEMBER 18

All creation testifies to your handiwork, Majestic Lord. Teach me to ponder the beauty before me in the promise of each new day: Christmas trees adorned with family treasures, the enticing aroma of cookies fresh out of the oven, festive visits from dear friends and family. Teach me to listen and to hear your whispers of delight as I consider the gifts of your hands. O God, I thank You that I am alive—alive in this beautiful world, alive on this magnificent day! And I praise and thank you for this company of faith that I call my friends, my brothers and sisters in Christ.

But the basic reality of God is plain enough. Open your eyes and there it is! By taking a long and thoughtful look at what God has created, people have always been able to see what their eyes as such can't see: eternal power, for instance, and the mystery of his divine being . . . Romans 1:19-20a (The Message)

What is the promise of this new day for me?

DECEMBER 19

O come, O come, Emmanuel, and still the endless chatter in my mind. Help me to give myself to You in this time of prayer. I pray that your light will illuminate all the corners of my being, so that I might be open to your will and your ways unfolding in my life. Thank you for this time of stillness, a haven in a frantically busy season where I can rest in your peace. Help me to listen for your whisper in the midst of life's competing voices. O Lord, may I rediscover the simplicity of the season as I remember again that the greatest gift is that You dwell with me every moment of every day.

How happy are those who have learned how to praise You;
  those *who journey through life* by the light of Your face.
Psalm 89:15 (The Voice)

Snowy Egret, Tampa, Florida

DECEMBER 20

O Loving Lord, help me to experience Christmas as a personal joy and also to give it away, unwrapped, by exuberant armfuls. Help me to share, dance, sing, and live Christmas with overflowing hands and sparkling eyes. Open my heart to the freshness of your love wrapped in the magic of a tiny baby, in Jesus Christ, my Lord.

Praise the LORD with melodies on the lyre;
make music for him on the ten-stringed harp.
Sing a new song of praise to him;
play skillfully on the harp, and sing with joy.
For the word of the LORD holds true,
and we can trust everything he does.
He loves whatever is just and good;
the unfailing love of the LORD fills the earth.
Psalm 33:2-5 (NLT)

Which Christmas carol touches my heart the most?

DECEMBER 21

Abba God, this Christmas, inspire me to look for the holy in the commonplace because that is where You seem to appear. Two thousand years ago, You blessed Mary and Joseph, a young couple in a darkened stable, and your glory shone on shepherds working in a forgotten field. And when I allow it, You come into my own familiar territory bringing the surprise of a resentment released, or a spirit lightened by generosity, or a sacred moment of truly being present with another human being. When that happens, Christ is born anew in me. Lord, I pray this year that some new heart will finally glimpse and be struck by your love through the gift of your Son. In that moment, all of heaven will rejoice.

That night there were shepherds staying in the fields nearby, guarding their flocks of sheep. Suddenly, an angel of the Lord appeared among them, and the radiance of the Lord's glory surrounded them. They were terrified, but the angel reassured them. "Don't be afraid!" he said. "I bring you good news that will bring great joy to all people. The Savior—yes, the Messiah, the Lord—has been born today in Bethlehem, the city of David! And you will recognize him by this sign: You will find a baby wrapped snugly in strips of cloth, lying in a manger."
Suddenly, the angel was joined by a vast host of others—the armies of heaven—praising God and saying,

> *"Glory to God in highest heaven,*
> *and peace on earth to those with whom God is pleased."*

When the angels had returned to heaven, the shepherds said to each other, "Let's go to Bethlehem! Let's see this thing that has happened, which the Lord has told us about."
They hurried to the village and found Mary and Joseph. And there was the baby, lying in the manger. After seeing him, the shepherds told everyone what had happened and what the angel had said to them about this child. Luke 2:8-17 (NLT)

The angels sing to me when . . .

Jupiter, Florida

DECEMBER 22

It's a funny thing about the Christmas season—memories come unbidden. I was sitting under the Christmas tree this week and began thinking about Christmases past. My mind traveled back to Fresno, California, where I was spending my first Christmas away from family. My roommate and I had no money, but we managed to get a tree with lights. And each day, we lit a candle and shared a Scripture reading to remind us of the meaning of Christmas. To this day, it is one of my favorite Christmas memories, probably because it was so simple. In fact I've learned it's the simple things that mean the most to me at Christmas.

Think about it this week when you're caught up in the hustle and bustle of it all. Snatch a few moments of quiet to remember the Prince of Peace.

O Emmanuel, who is God with us, give me a heart to hear the angels sing, sight to see the star when it begins to shine, and a life to live in joy at the wonder of it all.

After they had heard the king, they went on their way, and the star they had seen when it rose went ahead of them until it stopped over the place where the child was. When they saw the star, they were overjoyed. On coming to the house, they saw the child with his mother Mary, and they bowed down and worshiped him. Then they opened their treasures and presented him with gifts of gold, frankincense and myrrh. Matthew 2:9-11 (NIV)

DECEMBER 23

O Lord of this wondrous season, surrounded by creation's glory and the holiday decorations, we come together as your people. We bring our memories of Christmases past with us—some shiny and joy-tinged, others etched in bone-deep ache. Yet, in our congregation of faith, we come as a thankful people, singing of your grace. We come as a hungry people, longing to be filled. We come as a praying people, bringing our hopes and our joys. We come as a journeying people, seeking direction for our paths.

O Lord, who has spoken to your people throughout the ages, You speak to me most powerfully through the words and life of Jesus Christ. So, today, help me to hear your voice through prayer and silence, in music and message so that I might sense your presence in Emmanuel—God with us.

A voice of one calling:
"In the wilderness prepare
  the way for the LORD;
make straight in the desert
  a highway for our God.
Every valley shall be raised up,
  every mountain and hill made low;
the rough ground shall become level,
  the rugged places a plain.
And the glory of the LORD will be revealed,
  and all people will see it together.
    For the mouth of the LORD has spoken."
Isaiah 40:3-5 (NIV)

When do I sense God's presence most deeply at Christmastime?

DECEMBER 24

During a Christmas pageant a few years ago, a little boy named Connor tugged on my sleeve after the congregation sang "Silent Night", to tell me that the letters for "silent" were the same as "listen." Let's listen carefully in this pocket of silence.

O Lord of this Christmas Eve, amidst the twinkling joys of life and laughter, I give You thanks for the One whose birth I celebrate on this winter night. In this silent moment, I let go of the not-yet-done and the not-quite-perfect, to find a small patch of quiet and settle into the peace that only You can give. And when I do, I discover that You have been there all along, waiting for me to be still enough to notice your presence. Loving Lord, as my spirit yields to the spirit of your Son, may my Christmas be spent as a gift to those I love. Grant me the grace to so live this day in the name of Jesus so that someone would rediscover his face in mine.

Silent Night

Silent night, holy night!
All is calm, all is bright.
Round yon Virgin, Mother and Child.
Holy infant so tender and mild,
Sleep in heavenly peace,
Sleep in heavenly peace

Silent night, holy night!
Shepherds quake at the sight.
Glories stream from heaven afar
Heavenly hosts sing Alleluia,
Christ the Savior is born!
Christ the Savior is born
                    Joseph Mohr, 1816

DECEMBER 25

Gracious God, I celebrate You whose heart touches more than children at Christmas, rejoicing with me in my laughter, walking with me in my sorrow, and comforting me in my distress. I believe that the gift of the Christ child brings to my world both comfort and joy. It is my prayer on this most holy day that my life might glimpse possibility and hope in a world that shouts despair and struggle. Help me seek your comfort and enable me to be embraced by your joy, for then my life will reflect your grace. I pray in the name of Jesus, whose birth I celebrate today.

For to us a child is born,
*   to us a son is given,*
*   and the government will be on his shoulders.*
And he will be called
*   Wonderful Counselor, Mighty God,*
*   Everlasting Father, Prince of Peace.*
Isaiah 9:6-7 (NIV)

Poinsettia, Jupiter, Florida   Laurie Bohlke

DECEMBER 26

Almighty God, in this quiet moment You meet me before my day starts, while the morning is still fresh upon the earth. The Christmas excitement is over, and, for a moment, my life is paused; I am freed from the hectic pace of the holiday. I turn to You now with eagerness in my heart to celebrate your presence so that my love for You would be more than words and would instead give renewed purpose to my life. O Holy Spirit, Wind of heaven, touch my distracted life with power and grace as I invite You into my heart today.

Listen to my voice in the morning, LORD.
   Each morning I bring my requests to you and wait expectantly.
Psalm 5:3 (NLT)

I pause to feel the Holy Spirit in . . .

DECEMBER 27

O God, as I bring You my joys, I also bring my burdens. I open to You the frightened and uncertain places in my heart, the places within me that ring with questions, the parts that are pounded by doubts. I give You both the words of my mouth and the sighs of my heart. O Lord who abides with me daily, You pour out your blessing upon me. You call me by name, not because of what I might accomplish but because of who I am to You. You take the messes I have made in my life and weave them into a message of hope, not only for me but also for others who cross my path.

(Jesus said) *Do not let your hearts be troubled. You believe in God; believe also in me.* John 14:1 (NIV)

What are my messes that have become God's messages?

DECEMBER 28

O God of creation, You sprinkled the stars against the midnight sky; made the dry land and the seas, calling forth the quiet roar of surf on the sand; carved out the valleys; and raised the peaks of the mountain. O Gracious Master of all times and places and situations, whose footprints have tracked the world and whose heart embraces every human need, I still fill with wonder when I think that You know each person by name, and that You sent your Son to meet me in my hour of need.

May the LORD show you his favor
  and give you his peace.
Numbers 6:26 (NLT)

Mt. Shuksan, Washington

DECEMBER 29

Precious Lord, I feel a yearning for something more than the superficial life for which I so easily settle. You have planted within me the appetite for life in all its fullness, rooted and grounded in your grace. Sometimes I feel like a newcomer on this journey of faith, not knowing exactly where to begin. Yet, You reach out to me, asking me simply to knock on the door, to call out for your presence, for You have promised to meet me in my search for You.

And then, Gracious Father, make this world new through me. Change relationships through me. Heal wounds through me. Comfort weary spirits through me so that in my life the world might see the face of Jesus Christ.

(Jesus said) So I say to you: Ask and it will be given to you; seek and you will find; knock and the door will be opened to you. For everyone who asks receives; the one who seeks finds; and to the one who knocks, the door will be opened.
Luke 11: 9-10 (NIV)

I want to knock on the door and seek from God . . .

DECEMBER 30

Prince of Peace, for everything this day has brought, I give thanks—not alone for the beauty of the earth or for the splendor in these blazing blue skies jeweled by the morning sun, but also for the glory of these moments of quiet with You. How silently your peace steals into my heart, and with a sense of wonder, I feel your calm descending on my spirit.

Of one thing I am certain: my soul has become calm, quiet, *and contented in You*. . . Psalm 131:2a (The Voice)

When do I feel most calm and content?

DECEMBER 31

God of the ages, who was in the beginning, is here today with me, and will always be, I rest in your presence this day. I worship You who was there when the morning stars first sang together. I worship You who rides the winds of each day and promises me the gift of your presence in each new tomorrow. Thank you for life itself. Thank you for your mercy. Thank you for your forgiveness. Thank you for your amazing love.

"I am the Alpha and the Omega," says the Lord God, "who is, and who was, and who is to come, the Almighty." Revelation 1:8 (NIV)

Acadia National Park, Maine

It Is Well With My Soul

When peace like a river, attendeth my way,
When sorrows like sea billows roll;
Whatever my lot, Thou hast taught me to know,
It is well, it is well, with my soul.

Refrain:
It is well, (it is well),
With my soul, (with my soul)
It is well, it is well, with my soul.

Though Satan should buffet, though trials should come,
Let this blest assurance control,
That Christ has regarded my helpless estate,
And hath shed His own blood for my soul.

My sin, oh, the bliss of this glorious thought!
My sin, not in part but the whole,
Is nailed to the cross, and I bear it no more,
Praise the Lord, praise the Lord, O my soul!

For me, be it Christ, be it Christ hence to live:
If Jordan above me shall roll,
No pang shall be mine, for in death as in life,
Thou wilt whisper Thy peace to my soul.

But Lord, 'tis for Thee, for Thy coming we wait,
The sky, not the grave, is our goal;
Oh, trump of the angel! Oh, voice of the Lord!
Blessed hope, blessed rest of my soul

And Lord, haste the day when my faith shall be sight,
The clouds be rolled back as a scroll;
The trump shall resound, and the Lord shall descend,
Even so, it is well with my soul.

Horatio Spafford, 1873